EMILY DICKINSON

Daisies, Clovers and Buttercups, by C. M. Badger.
(Reproduced by permission of the Houghton
Library, Harvard University.)

"EMILY DICKINSON
Woman Poet"

PAULA BENNETT

University of Iowa Press, Iowa City

Copyright © 1990 by Paula Bennett

University of Iowa Press, Iowa City 52242

International Standard Book Number 0-87745-310-1 paper

Library of Congress Catalog Card Number 90-70742

Printed in the United States of America

96 95 94 93 92   P   5 4 3 2

To my students
and
in memoriam
Thomas P. McDonnell
litterateur and friend

Contents

Acknowledgments

First I wish to acknowledge my debt to the many feminist scholars of Dickinson but, in particular, to those women scholars who first broke ground for lesbian studies of Dickinson: Rebecca Patterson, Jeannette Foster, and Lillian Faderman. Their honesty and courage has made our work—and lives—richer.

I also gratefully acknowledge the careful editorial work and sharp critical commentary provided by J.S., Martha Nell Smith, Susan R. Solberg, and Carolyn Swift. The attention they gave this manuscript in its various stages went well beyond what any author has a right to expect from her friends. A special thank you to Jane Langton for her encouragement and for giving the book such a close reading in its final days—and to J.S. for first pointing out 'Forbidden Fruit' to me, oh so many years ago and, more recently, for giving me 'As if I asked a common Alms' in its current construction. For reading individual chapters and providing advice and encouragement, thank you to Annie Finch,

Linda Gardiner, Jackie Lapidus, and Eve Kosofsky Sedgwick.

My gratitude also goes to the Houghton Library, Harvard University, for giving me permission to examine the individual Dickinson holographs cited in this text and to Beth Kiley of the permissions department of Harvard University Press for being so understanding and helpful regarding my special needs at a time when she was already inundated with work. To Jackie Jones of Harvester Wheatsheaf there are not thanks enough. She knows why.

Finally, I wish to thank the students of my Dickinson course at University College, Northeastern University, who over the years have deepened my understanding of her poems and my love for the poet. This is their book.

Credits

A Note on the Dickinson Texts

Only a handful of Dickinson's poems were published in her lifetime, and most of these were published without her consent. This means that textual authority for the poetry resides in the holographs alone. *All* published versions of Dickinson's poems, even those in critical texts such as this, represent editorial revisions. Except where an existing fair copy takes clear precedence, I have based my texts whenever possible on the Franklin facsimiles, otherwise on the Johnson variorum edition. In transcribing the facsimiles, I have kept Dickinson's lineation and her method of indicating variants with a cross (+). Insofar as possible, I have also placed the variants as she did. However, since this is not a study of the manuscripts *per se* (and since they are much more difficult matters to determine and reproduce accurately), I have made no attempt to keep her margins or spacing or to indicate the length or slant of her dashes and the other peculiarities of her punctuation. As Susan Howe has argued, for an appreciation of the 'open processual'

character of Dickinson's writing, these 'accidentals'—
many of which may well *not* be accidental—must be
studied in full, but a book of this length in a series such as
this is not the place to do so.

In transcribing from the Johnson edition, I follow the
editor's format, including his regularization of Dickin-
son's poetic line and his use of line numbers to indicate
variants. In all cases of quotation, whether from the fac-
similes, the holographs, the edited poems, or Johnson's
edition of the letters, I have retained Dickinson's idio-
syncratic spelling and grammar. In Chapter 1, I discuss
the effect our editorial decisions have on our reading of
the variants, in particular.

Introduction

Between 1848 and 1849, two anthologies of women's poetry were published in America: *The American Female Poets*, edited by Caroline May, and *The Female Poets of America*, edited by Rufus Griswold. May's volume includes 81 poets, beginning with Anne Bradstreet (1612) and Jane Turell (1708) and ending with a sizeable group of writers whose careers commence in the late 1840s. Griswold's volume is somewhat larger (96 poets) and more intellectually pretentious, but covers an identical range. On the whole, the same poets appear in both volumes, sometimes with the same poems.

The vast majority of the poets published in these two anthologies came of age between 1830 and 1845. Needless to say, Emily Dickinson does not appear among them. But she must have been aware of their existence for, as a group (along with their sisters in fiction), they were among the most popular and prolific writers of polite literature in her day. As Cheryl Walker has cogently argued, some grasp of the literary phenomenon

1

they represent is necessary, therefore, to an appreciation of Dickinson's work and, in particular, to an understanding of how she defined herself as a woman poet, and how she positioned herself in respect to America's literary traditions.[1]

The situation of the nineteenth-century woman poet in the United States was a paradox. On the one hand, women's poetry had at last achieved a real degree of success within the culture at large. Poems by women not only graced the pages of local newspapers and women's magazines, but appeared regularly in such prestigious literary journals as *Graham's Magazine* and *The Atlantic Monthly*. Well-known male literary figures such as Griswold, Poe, and Thomas Wentworth Higginson actively sponsored women poets. Some women poets, like Helen Hunt Jackson, had become figures of esteem with wide cultural influence. Indeed, one poem by a woman, 'The Battle Hymn of the Republic,' published in the February, 1862, issue of *The Atlantic Monthly*, can fairly be said to have summed up for many the spirit of the age.

Yet, at the same time, aside from Jackson (much of whose reputation was based on her prose works), few women poets appear to have taken their publication to heart as evidence that their work had attained professional status. On the contrary. Even those writers, like Lydia Huntley Sigourney, who earned their living by their pens tended to disavow professionalism both for themselves and their work. For the majority—the homebound women whose poems on love, duty, nature and God filled local newspapers and magazines—writing was little more than an extension of domestic life, a putting into words of the values they held most dear.

Mrs Swift, Caroline May writes of one poet appearing in her anthology, 'now resides in Easton, Pennsylvania, where, for many years past, she has been confined to one house, almost to one room, by the illness of her husband. Her poems frequently appear in Neal's Saturday Gazette; but they are written less for the public than for a circle of warmly-attached friends. A vein of tenderness runs through them all.'[2] Similarly, Jessie G. M'Cartee 'is entirely unknown to the literary world, never having . . . imprinted her poetry anywhere except in the hearts of her family, and now and then in the pages of a country newspaper. . . .' She lives, May tells us, in Goshen, New York, 'quietly and meekly fulfilling her responsible duties as a minister's wife, and the mother of a very large family' (May 151). Of Mrs Easling, an established poet, May reports that she has never 'left her home for a greater distance than forty miles, or for a longer period than forty-eight hours. Well,' the anthologist concludes, 'may such a nestling bird sing sweetly of home's quiet joys' (May 328).

Sentimentalized as such biographies are, they also indicate that neither the poets—nor their anthologist— were prepared to stake a serious claim for women in writing as a profession. Those poets who, like Sigourney, did turn to writing in order to make a living, did so, as a rule, because their husbands failed to provide. Dedicated to poetry though they were, the autonomy of art escaped them. Even Helen Hunt Jackson, who insisted after marriage that she be given freedom to write, still claimed that motherhood was woman's most important creative activity, and still put the great bulk of her production in the service of others.[3]

If the professional aspirations of these poets were limited by their situation as women in the nineteenth century, their poetry was equally affected. Generally speaking, nineteenth-century American poetry, whether by men or women, is more conservative than the prose. Aside from Whitman, there are no male poets to rival Poe, Thoreau, Hawthorne or Melville. And, as David Reynolds has recently pointed out in his study of popular literature in this period, *Beneath the American Renaissance*, with the exception of Dickinson, no woman poet raises the kinds of social and religious questions one finds in the works of Fanny Fern (Sara Parton), Harriet Spofford and others.[4]

Given the restrictions on middle-class women's social role, however, the consequences for women's poetry of this innately conservative tendency were inevitably more severe than they were for the poetry of men. Typically conventional in style and theme and deeply infused with the sentimentality that characterizes the era, the poetry of mid-nineteenth-century American women inscribes the domestic ideology that shaped their lives. Denying any interest in fame (even when they secretly longed for it), these poets focus on the duties and obligations, the joys and sorrows, of domestic existence. They celebrate life's small triumphs and God's great beneficence. They write feelingly of their faith, their beliefs, their hopes and fears, and—sometimes—of their resentments. Less frequently but always passionately, they champion the rights of the Indians, the enslaved, or the otherwise downtrodden. As May says in her biography of Sigourney, their 'one great aim' was '*to do good*' (May 77). In the world in which they found themselves, their ministrations were much desired.

By 1848, the combined forces of the industrial and the commercial revolutions and the growth of urban centers had changed the face of America. With the breakup of a stable agrarian economy, the church lost much of its hold over the individual citizen's life. Indeed, the church itself was ridden with factionalism and theological dispute. According to Ann Douglas, women writers, together with male sentimentalists and disestablished clergymen, rose to fill the gap.[5] Discomfited or, perhaps, frightened by the social changes occurring around it, bourgeois culture wanted and needed the hope-filled brand of religious enthusiasm these women offered, the lays of sacred and desexualized love, the inspirational outpourings on nature and life.

Nineteenth-century American women poets met this demand with ream after ream of highly accessible and highly nostalgic verse. In their hands, *belles-lettres* became a tool to ease the painful conflicts that had opened up between Christian values and the social realities of nineteenth-century life. This is true even of the more socially sophisticated writers. Here, for example, is Sigourney, one of the most popular poets of her day, on an absent daughter. (With the waning of the multifunctional farm family, the separation of parents and children had become an issue at this time.)

Where art thou, bird of song?
    Brightest one and dearest?
Other groves among,
    Other nests thou cheerest;
Sweet thy warbling skill
    To each ear that heard thee,
But 'twas sweetest still
    To the heart that rear'd thee.
. . . . .
Seek thy Saviour's flock,
    To his blest fold going,
Seek that smitten rock
    Whence our peace is flowing;
Still should Love rejoice,
    Whatso'er betide thee,
If that Shepherd's voice
    Evermore might guide thee.
                                        (May 85 and 86)

And here is Elizabeth Oakes-Smith, another poet of formidable reputation, on an April rain:

> The cottage door is open wide,
> > And cheerful sounds are heard;
> The young girl sings at the merry wheel
> > A song like the wildwood bird;
> The creeping child by the old worn sill
> > Peers out with winking eye,
> And his ringlets parts with his chubby hand,
> > As the drops come spattering by.
> . . . . .
> Ay, shout away, ye joyous throng!
> > For yours is the April day;
> I love to see your spirits dance,
> > In your pure and healthful play.
> > > > > (May 278)

Unlike Mrs Swift and Mrs Easling, both Sigourney and Oakes-Smith led public lives. Besides being a best-selling author, Sigourney wrote for various political causes including temperance and the Greek War Relief Fund. The victim of a forced marriage, Oakes-Smith actively participated in literary salons in the late 1840s and went on to become a noted feminist lecturer. But in poems such as the above, their knowledge of the world (and indeed of their own personal struggles), is erased. When it came to women's poetry, 'warm domestic affection, and pure religious feeling' (May 115) were what was wanted and by and large, this is what these writers provide, making themselves—as one writer put it (May 170)—'Aeolian harps' to the cultural values of their age. As Walker admonishes, one must read 'with a good deal of care,' to hear in the subtext of their work the burgeoning within them of more ambitious and less ingenuous notions.[6] On the

6

surface, at any rate, they were prepared to renounce, accommodate and reflect.

Walker's argument for the subtext of discontent in women's poetry is persuasively stated and convincing. However, it does not alter the fact that for these poets— as for middle-class women generally in mid-nineteenth-century culture—conventional ideology was a primary source of identity as well as strength. The 'True Woman,' Carroll Smith-Rosenberg writes, was the invention of the nineteenth-century bourgeoisie. 'Domestic, Dependent, Pure and Pious, [she] constituted the mirror image of the Common Man, noted for his self-reliance, talent, and competitiveness.'[7] By the middle of the century, women, according to popular culture, had become the repositories of the moral and spiritual values which men, in their quest for material success, were rapidly leaving behind. Middle-class women generally embraced this newly-constructed definition of their role with *élan*. Indeed, they gloried in it. For, whatever its limitations, it gave them a definite and unimpeachable sphere in which to exercise power—the home. And, equally important, it made them, as David Reynolds asserts, moral exemplars to the culture at large.[8]

'[L]earn to love . . . home,' a minister's wife exhorts young ladies in the January, 1851, issue of *The Mothers' Journal and Family Visitant*, a veritable storehouse of popular wisdom, 'let all your accomplishments and affectionate attentions cluster about that sanctum of the heart, rendering it a paradise of real joy and consolation.'[9] In a letter to her mother, Mary Lyon, the formidable founder of Mount Holyoke (where Dickinson spent her one college year), says that the most important training she can give her students is, finally, domestic. 'O how immensely important is this work of preparing the daughters of the land to be good mothers!' she exclaims.[10]

Lyon's conviction regarding the importance of her mission reflects her culture's point of view. According to the wisdom of the day, women were different from men—more elevated, more pure, more instinctively religious—and to their lot fell, consequently, the preservation of humanity's moral and spiritual well-being. 'As a companion or associate [woman] moulds [men's] characters to an assimilation with her own,' writes 'Cousin Robert' in *The Mother's Journal*. 'If she is intelligent and virtuous, if she is pious and refined, she will have an elevating, moral, and refining influence upon all with whom she associates. All that is noble in the character of man is attributable to the influence of woman. Man forms his character from female influence.'[11]

Women took such words to heart. They were the ones whom God had ordained to serve mankind's spiritual as well as physical needs, and this service was one that humanity (or, at any rate, American men) could not do without. If, for a great many women, this definition of their role meant immersing themselves entirely within the home—like Emily Dickinson's mother, leading lives of quiet desperation as they 'meekly' fulfilled their responsible duties—for others, the ideal of domestic service was unquestionably liberating.[12] Not only did it encourage women to pursue a variety of 'service' careers (teaching, nursing, missionary work and writing—as they defined it), but it also led to women's participation in the temperance and abolition movements and finally—however ironically—it led to the struggle for women's rights.

In every instance, it was the domestic code of 'service to others' ('doing good') that was the controlling justification for and impetus behind women's actions. *Uncle Tom's Cabin*, a book of unquestioned political impact, if arguable artistic merit, represents the literary apogee of this ideal. As Jane Tompkins has recently argued, in this novel, dying becomes the ultimate act of heroic self-sacrifice, and writing about such self-sacrifice, the high road to female political and textual power.[13] This was not, however, a social ideal—or a point of view on literary power—that Emily Dickinson espoused, and it is indicative that Dickinson never mentions this phenomenally successful work or its author in her writing. Indeed, with the exception of Jackson and Spofford, Dickinson barely mentions American women writers at all.

Emily Dickinson's relationship to the woman's sphere and to the literature that sprang from it is in many ways the subject of this book; but it is a difficult and complex relationship, one that is not easily defined and that is riddled with obvious and not so obvious contradictions. On the one hand, as Walker and others have observed, Dickinson appears to have lived the epitome of a conventional mid-nineteenth-century middle-class woman's life.[14] Indeed, outwardly, Dickinson's life was a model (or, perhaps, a parody) of domesticity. Like Mrs Swift and Mrs Easling, she was so devoted to her household duties and obligations (her garden, kitchen, and parents), that she never left home. Only the fact that she did not marry distinguishes her from them.

In spirit, also, Dickinson's public persona seems to fit what the 'True Woman' was supposed to be, especially as this woman was incarnated in her role as 'poetess,' in Cheryl Walker's words, 'intense, spontaneous, effusive, ethereal.'[15] To her niece, Martha Dickinson Bianchi (as to Helen Hunt Jackson), the poet resembled a large white moth. To Thomas Wentworth Higginson, a pattering child. To Joseph Lyman, a figure too rare and spiritous to kiss: 'a spirit clad in white, figure so draped as to be misty[,] face moist, translucent alabaster, forehead firmer as of statuary marble.' Her mouth, he declared in this late—and highly gothicized—portrait (written after he left Amherst), was 'made for nothing & used for nothing but uttering choice speech, rare . . . thoughts, glittering, starry misty . . . figures, winged words.'[16]

For those acquainted with her poetry, this view of Dickinson-the-poetess tended to carry over into their reading of her poems as well. Emily Fowler Ford, a contemporary and former schoolmate, found Dickinson's poems *so* ethereal she advised Dr Holland against publishing them: '"They are beautiful, so concentrated, but they remind me of orchids, air-plants that have no roots in earth".'[17] For the cover of Dickinson's first book of poems, Mabel Loomis Todd could think of nothing more appropriate than a drawing of Indian pipes, a white leafless saprophyte that survives on decayed matter. Far more important, as Martha Nell Smith has argued, the selection and editing of Dickinson's poems also fit Todd's and Higginson's presuppositions about the author's life and their desire to present her in the mold of a 'poetess.'[18] Textualized in the early editions of Dickinson's poems, this image of the poet and this interpretation of her work still lingers in the popular mind—and possibly in the minds of some critics.

Yet for all the 'etherealness' of her public persona, Dickinson herself appears to have had little sympathy with the values of spirituality, purity and service underlying the role she chose to play. In one of her more caustic comments, she reports to her cousin, Louise Norcross, that she burnt a letter from a 'Miss P—' (possibly Elizabeth Stuart Phelps). 'She wrote me in October, requesting me to aid the world by my chirrup more. . . . I replied declining. She did not write to me again—she might have been offended, or perhaps is extricating humanity from some hopeless ditch . . .' (L,500).

And in her poetry, Dickinson could be equally acerbic. In 'What Soft—Cherubic Creatures,' she attacks her female peers for their hypocritical over-refinement respecting sexual matters. 'One would,' she declares, with a hostility that is startling even in her, 'as soon assault/a Plush—/Or violate a Star'[19] as make love to one of them. In 'She rose to His Requirement,' a far more compassionate but no less angry poem, Dickinson laments the fate of the woman who (like her mother) buries her talent (her 'Gold') in a domestic life:

> She rose to His Requirement—
> dropt
> The Playthings of Her Life
> To take the honorable
> Work
> Of Woman, and of Wife—
>
> If ought She missed
> in Her new Day,
> Of Amplitude, or Awe—
> Or first Prospective—Or
> the Gold
> In using, wear away,
>
> It lay unmentioned—as
> the Sea
> Develope Pearl, and Weed,
> But only to Himself—be
> known
> The Fathoms they abide—
>
> (#732, F,937)

The immediate source of 'She rose to His Requirement'

is Ariel's song in *The Tempest*; but unlike the transformation which the lost father undergoes in Shakespeare's magic lyric, the 'sea change' which the wife (mother) experiences in Dickinson's poem is only ironically a form of rebirth. It does not lead to an enhanced or more valuable being: e.g., 'Those are pearls that were his eyes' (I.ii. 399). Instead, the wife's 'Gold' is worn away and her hopes (her 'first Prospective') are drowned in the silence and obscurity of the marital sea. If anything comes of them, whether pearl or weed, only the husband knows. To the world, she might as well be dead.

Whether or not 'She rose to His Requirement' is actually about Dickinson's mother, the awareness which the poet shows in it of domesticity's dangers (in particular, its threat to self) was crucial. While other nineteenth-century women writers complained, at times bitterly, against domestic restraints, few managed to avoid them as successfully as Dickinson. Motherhood, Jane Eberwein shrewdly observes, is one role Dickinson never fantasizes for herself.[20] Despite her apparently strong attachment to a 'Master' figure in the early 1860s, and to Judge Otis P. Lord later in life, wifehood had almost as little appeal to the poet, and service to others none at all. 'I dont keep the Moth part of the House—I keep the Butterfly part' (L,924), Dickinson comments in one prose fragment, airily placing the burden of household duties on the obliging backs of others. Although she did her share of household chores, her position was one to which her family seems to have acceded. 'Emily,' her sister Vinnie declared, 'was a very busy person herself. She had to think—she was the only one of us who had that to do.'[21]

Interpreted in this light, the extremes to which Dickinson carried her 'poetess' persona—'moist,' 'translucent,' 'misty'—may have been less a yielding to nineteenth-century feminine values than a protection against the actual rigors of a nineteenth-century middle-class woman's everyday life. 'It must be borne in mind,' May writes, 'that not many ladies in this country are permitted sufficient leisure from the cares and duties of home to devote themselves, either from choice, or as a means of living, to literary pursuits' (May vi). After a tumultuous period in adolescence during which Dickinson fought the battle of housework with her mother, she appears to have won this leisure, largely by taking 'the Butterfly part.' As Lyman's reverential reaction to Dickinson's persona suggests, her role-playing may also have protected her against any man presumptuous enough to want to pursue her in marriage. Certainly, Lyman found her too 'pure' to kiss.

Yet even if this is true, it is also true, as a number of feminist scholars have insisted, that there is no way we can separate Dickinson from the domestic life she led or from the role of 'poetess' she chose to play. Indeed, to do so can only distort our reading of the poet. For whatever reservations Dickinson had concerning domesticity, all the evidence suggests that she nevertheless identified strongly with women and with many aspects of domestic life, including many of the tasks she performed (cooking and gardening, in particular). Her submergence into the woman's sphere and her presentation of herself as 'poetess' (a *woman* poet) was, therefore, a good deal more than simply a role she played in order to keep from playing others. Paradoxical though it may seem—as for women poets generally in her period—Dickinson's domesticity was also, to use Sandra Gilbert's term, the central 'mystery' (ritual, secret rite, art, enigma) of her life.[22] If her treatment of domestic themes differs radically at times from that of her peers, domesticity itself was nevertheless central to her identity as poet and to her matter and style.

Largely as a consequence of feminist scholarship, the importance of Dickinson's commitment to domesticity and, in particular, the significance of her feelings for women, has come into focus in recent years.[23] Like most nineteenth-century women, the poet not only lived her entire life 'at home,' but spent her life largely in a circle of women—her sister Vinnie, Mrs Holland, the Norcross cousins, and her sister-in-law Susan Gilbert Dickinson, to name the most important. These were the individuals upon whom she depended for emotional support and to whom she opened up most fully in her letters. Her relationships with them were intense, satisfying, and, as we shall see in the last chapter, in some instances, unequivocally erotic.

'Vinnie,' the poet declares, 'has been Soldier and Angel too since our Parents died, and only carries a "drawn Sword" in behalf of Eden' (L,794). 'Where my Hands are cut, Her fingers will be found inside,' Dickinson writes of Susan in 1864 (L,430). In 1878, she says that Sue has made Heaven 'a sterile stimulus' (L,631). Such statements may seem hyperbolic, but they were rooted in realities. Based on shared domestic values, especially the values of mutuality and nurturance, Dickinson's relationships with women sustained and protected her throughout her life. Her last written message, 'Called back' (L,906) was sent to the Norcross cousins. They are the words that now appear on her tombstone.

Equally important, Dickinson's definition of herself as woman poet was also rooted in her positive feelings for women. If, with the exception of Jackson, Dickinson never mentions American women poets by name, she nevertheless saw herself as part of a female literary tradition which she and they shared. British in origin, this tradition had found its richest, most complicated, expression in the work of Elizabeth Barrett Browning, the Brontë sisters, and George Eliot. And in it, Dickinson took great pride. 'What do I think of *Middlemarch*,' she declares to the Norcross cousins, 'What do I think of glory—' (L,506). Emily Brontë is 'gigantic Emily Brontë' (L,721). Most beloved of all, Elizabeth Barrett Browning's poetry produces a 'Conversion of the Mind.'

As Dickinson indicates in a poèm dedicated to Barrett Browning, she was so strongly drawn to the British authors because they expanded cultural definitions of how a woman could write and, therefore, what a 'poetess' could be. As a result, their work was liberating for the Amherst poet in a way that the work of fellow American poets could not be. By limiting their professional aspirations, and by failing to question openly the more oppressive aspects of domestic ideology in their writing— if not necessarily in their lives—women poets in the United States had, in effect, accepted their 'small' size. The British writers, on the other hand, had not. To Dickinson, they were oaks who had outgrown their flowerpots, 'bees' the size of 'butterflies':

I think I was enchanted
When first a +sombre Girl—
I read that Foreign Lady—
The Dark—felt beautiful—

And whether it was noon
at night—
Or only Heaven—at Noon—
For very Lunacy of Light
I had not power to tell—

The Bees—became as
Butterflies—
The Butterflies—as +Swans—
Approached—and spurned

the narrow Grass—
And just the +meanest Tunes

That Nature murmured to
herself
To keep herself in Cheer—
I took for Giants—practising
Titanic Opera—

The Days—to Mighty Metres
stept—
The Homeliest—adorned
As if unto a +Jubilee
'Twere suddenly +Confirmed—

I could not have defined the
change—
Conversion of the Mind
Like Sanctifying in the Soul—
Is Witnessed—not Explained—

'Twas a Divine Insanity—
The +Danger to be sane
Should I again experience—
'Tis Antidote to turn—

To Tomes of solid Witchcraft—
Magicians be asleep—
But Magic—hath an Element
Like Deity—to keep—

+little Girl   +As Moons—
lit up the low—inferior Grass—
+Common Tunes—faintest—
+Sacrament   +ordained   +Sorrow
(#593, F,689–91)

In *The Nightingale's Burden*, Cheryl Walker observes that 'During this phase of American women's history, it is hard to find a woman expressing pride in her success.'[24]

16

Albeit with irony, Sigourney depicts her 'muse' as a
kitchen wench on Mount Parnassus, 'a woman of all
work, and an aproned waiter.'[25] The first time a poem of
hers appeared in print with her name on it, Caroline
Gilman cried half the night. 'Later,' Walker records, 'she
admitted to being "as alarmed as if I had been detected in
man's apparel".'[26] Although (like Sigourney) Gilman
went on to enjoy an extensive public career—with titles
such as *Recollections of a New-England Housekeeper* and
Recollections of a Southern Matron—only 'doing good'
(serving others), could possibly justify such presump-
tion on a woman's part. To these poets, writing well was
not its own excuse—not here—or on Parnassus.

Given the ubiquitousness of this kind of apologia, its
very absence from Dickinson's poem on Barrett Brown-
ing is telling. What concerns Dickinson is not the 'good'
Barrett Browning does with her writing, but how
effective—as writing—Barrett Browning's poetry is.
Reading 'that Foreign Lady' changes the speaker's per-
ception of the world and her place in it. Nature's
'meanest Tunes' (lowest and most '*homely*' become
'Titanic Opera,' with its pun on Latin, 'works.' Bees are
butterflies, and butterflies are swans. Size is no longer a
restraint, nor is place. These newly-spawned creatures
spurn 'the narrow Grass,' rising above the 'narrow' cir-
cumference of earth-bound female domesticity and chal-
lenging its 'low' or 'inferior' state. With this challenge, a
new world of possibility opens up for the home-bound
American poet.

'Could I make you and Austin—proud—sometime—a
great way off—'twould give me taller feet,' Dickinson
wrote Sue in 1861, in response to her sister-in-law's
enthusiastic praise for 'Safe in their Alabaster Chambers'
(L,380). The poet was playing on her meter, but she
was also playing on her size and situation. Given the

inhibiting social restrictions on women in the United States—and the restrictions on her own life—for Dickinson to be 'gigantic' (that is, tall and 'Mighty' like Barrett Browning or Brontë) would be no mean feat. She needed a 'Conversion of the Mind' to believe that she could be.

In 'I think I was enchanted,' Dickinson claims that reading Barrett Browning's works produced this conversion. They cured her of the poisonous, but presumably rational, belief that women—like butterflies and bees—actually were what her culture perceived them to be—small, earth-bound, and powerless (without magic). In the tangled web of the poem's imagery, Dickinson identifies her moment of conversion with a 'Jubilee.' That is, she identifies it with the celebration which the ancient Hebrews held after their emancipation from slavery. To be a woman as women were socially-constructed *was* to be enslaved, and to be liberated from this construct, a true 'Lunacy of Light.' For it meant viewing her womanhood and herself as woman poet in a new way, a way that made noon of night and small things great. It meant, in other words, an end to the (presumably rational) darkness in which female light was sunk.[27]

Dickinson's poem on Barrett Browning, like her other statements on the British women writers, indicates that she saw herself specifically as a woman poet, but a woman poet of a different kind. Like the British women writers, she wanted to stretch the boundaries of what it meant to be a woman and to write in a womanly way. In this book I will explore how this desire informs Dickinson's relationship to the social, religious and intellectual currents of her time. In particular, I will look at how it shaped her poetry, freeing her to handle the traditional genres of women's verse in ways that they had never been handled before.

As the early presentation of her poems suggests, Dickinson wrote on the usual topics for nineteenth-century American women's poetry: 'Life,' 'Love,' 'Nature,' 'Time and Eternity.' However inadequate such theme-based categories seem to us, they are basic to her writing and attest to the profound influence other American women poets had upon her. Studying Dickinson's handling of these conventional lyric genres against that of her peers will make this influence clear in ways that Walker, who focuses primarily on the Nightingale theme, has not done. As in her life, where she played the role of 'poetess' with a difference, so in her poetry, Dickinson both was and was not a 'woman poet' in the American mould. Like her biography, her poetry cannot be fairly separated from its cultural context, especially the context other women's poetry provides.

The first chapter lays the groundwork for this discussion by exploring the metaphysical basis for Dickinson's intellectual and linguistic experimentation and in particular for the disjunctions which, as Cristanne Miller argues, characterize her thought and style. Dickinson's anomic (or illegal) poetics reflect the poet's rejection of past masculinist 'truth.' The world which her poetry creates is a world in which nothing can be known for certain and in which, therefore, the ideals of order and perfection (the foundation stones of Western phallocentrism) give way to process and incompletion. The result is a free, constantly changing form of poetry in which conclusions—whether formal or thematic—cannot be drawn and in which *variant readings are part of the very substance of the text*.

The second chapter looks at the way Dickinson uses her intellectual and poetic freedom to challenge traditional religious beliefs, especially those that cluster about the concept of a transcendent male deity—a sovereign God.

Dickinson lived in a period when traditional articles of faith had been 'softened' to accommodate a more feminized, benevolent version of God. But this softening produced logical dilemmas of its own. In her poetry, she twists the strands of Puritan and sentimental concepts of God into a critique of both. Her religious poetry is at once an exploration of key ideas: death, immortality and the nature of God, and a protest, vehement and passionate, against the values androcentric religion encodes, whether in its Calvinist or more sentimentalized form.

Dickinson's nature poetry is the subject of the third chapter. Unable to reconcile herself to the concept of a transcendent God, Dickinson presents nature as a woman-centered and materially-based alternative to established religion. More deeply embedded in women's culture than any other aspect of her work, Dickinson's nature poetry reflects the poet's profound need to go outside the masculinist tradition in order to find sources of power that are specifically female and specifically her own. In her close observation of nature and her intense, almost mystical response to its physical beauty, Dickinson found the power and healing, the 'Bliss,' she sought.

Chapter 4 discusses Dickinson's psychological poetry, her poetry of 'Life.' Like other women poets of her period, Dickinson used her poetry to transcribe her 'heart's record.' But the indeterminacy of her psychological poetry has created serious problems of interpretation. This chapter explores the way in which Dickinson's use of indeterminacy enriches our reading of her poetry, even as it obscures her poems' biographical roots. By viewing this poetry within the context of nineteenth-century women's poetry generally, its relevance to her life can nevertheless be established, albeit not in a specific (or one-to-one) way.

The final chapter returns to the issue of gender and

genre. In this chapter, Dickinson's patterns of erotic imagery are examined for what they tell us both about Dickinson's sexuality and her attitude toward female sexual and creative power. These patterns indicate that both Dickinson's sexuality and her imagination were homoerotic and autoerotic. Moreover, they support the idea that this female-centered eroticism was one of the primary enabling factors in Dickinson's emergence as a strong woman poet. In defining both her sexuality and her creativity as a 'little' but explosive 'force,' Dickinson gives voice to the clitorocentrism that, I argue, is fundamental to her work.

Throughout this study, I have drawn extensively on recent feminist criticism of Dickinson and nineteenth-century American women's culture. However, there are certain basic assumptions governing my approach which, because they are subject to controversy, should be established from the outset. First, and most important, there are no hard data proving that Dickinson's life was unhappy, unfulfilled, or (aside from some eye trouble) limited in any substantive way.[28] She did go through periods of severe stress, as we all do. But by the time she reached her forties, her letters indicate that she had achieved a full and satisfied maturity and was totally cognizant of her enormous powers. Her life may seem limited to us, but by nineteenth-century standards for American middle-class women, it was an extraordinarily free one. As Adrienne Rich argues, for Dickinson, freedom was everything, and the self-imposed restrictions of her life worked paradoxically to ensure that freedom (of the kind that mattered to her most) was what she had.[29]

Secondly, this book assumes that Dickinson's love for her sister-in-law, Susan Gilbert Dickinson, not her relatively brief involvement with the Master (if, indeed, such a person existed), is the central emotional experience of the poet's life. The privileging of the Master episode in Dickinson criticism has seriously distorted our reading of the poet's life and work. In particular, it has obscured the significance of Dickinson's homoeroticism to both. By illuminating the richness and beauty of the homoerotic strain in Dickinson's writing, both in her nature poetry and in her erotic poetry, I hope to put her relationships to men, and to 'masculine' concepts such as God and death, in a new perspective and to establish Dickinson's love for women as the strong positive force it is in her work. Homoeroticism was not just a matter of sexuality for the poet. It was a point of view. And her love of women and things female·affects everything she wrote.

Finally, while I have tried to address a number of important issues which theoreticians have raised, in particular, those around female sexuality and female creativity, this book is not a theoretically-oriented study. My first and chief aim is to help make Dickinson accessible to teachers, students, and general readers. My second is to show how—by placing her poetry within the context created by other American women poets—we can understand her for what she was—a nineteenth-century American 'woman poet' of a different kind: a poet who both drew from and critiqued the work of her peers. In neither case was a strictly theoretical approach warranted. Indeed, it might well have hindered these objectives.

To an extent unique among lyric poets in the Anglo-American tradition, Dickinson was the creator of her own discourse. She cannot be de-centered as the subject of her verse, nor can her subjectivity be separated from her complicated and in many ways idiosyncratic response to her situation as a mid-nineteenth-century woman, without radically affecting our reading of her poetry and obscuring many of the gains it achieves.[30] Cut from the framework provided by her life and, in particular, by her situation as a woman in her period, the indeterminacy of her poetry can only work against itself. Her writing will seem as totally inward and fragmented as some linguistically-oriented critics claim it to be. By establishing the literary, social and biographical contexts for Dickinson's poetry, I hope to reverse this impression.

At a period when, it seems, virtually every woman poet in the United States failed to rise above the limitations imposed on women's poetry by women's complicity in a system that oppressed them, Emily Dickinson sought 'taller feet.' Given her native ability as a writer, what is extraordinary is not that she attained them, but that she was able to retain a positive and fulfilling sense of womanhood while she did. How she could, and the effect this has upon her poetry, is what this book is about.

Chapter One

Beyond the Dip of Bell

I used to spell the one by that name *"Fee Bee"* when a Child, and have seen no need to improve! Should I spell all the things as they sounded to me, and say all the facts as I saw them, it would send consternation among more than the *"Fee Bees"*!

(Dickinson to Mrs Holland, 1883)

In 1862, Emily Dickinson asked Thomas Wentworth Higginson whether or not her poetry was publishable. He informed her that her 'gait' (meter) was ' "spasmodic" ' and her writing ' "uncontrolled" ' (L,409). He told her what she needed to know.

Dickinson had selected her 'Preceptor' with care. Higginson's 'Letter to a Young Contributor,' encouraging new poets like herself to submit their wares, had just appeared in *The Atlantic Monthly*. No less important, three years before, he had published in the same journal 'Ought Women to Learn the Alphabet,' a passionate defense of women's right to an education. A freethinker and activist in the cause of civil rights, Higginson had concluded this scathing attack on nineteenth-century chauvinistic attitudes with high praise for Elizabeth Barrett Browning, Emily Dickinson's favorite woman poet. If her own poetry was going to be acceptable to any member of America's literary establishment, it would be to this man. It was not. Although a handful of Dickinson's poems were published during her lifetime—some with, most probably without her permission—she did not try seriously for acceptance again. But neither did she change the way she wrote.

Dickinson's gender was not the reason for her unpublishability in the nineteenth century. Her writing was. By the second half of the century, the art of poetry in the United States was virtually dead. Weighted down by convention in language and theme, and filled with bromides for religion and life, American poetry had suffered the same fate as many other aspects of middle-class American culture. In Ann Douglas's term, it had become 'feminized': sentimental, soft.[1] Douglas's choice of terminology notwithstanding, however, women were not the only ones whose poetry exhibited these qualities. The work of artists presumably cut from nobler stuff was also infected, as Emerson's frequently-anthologized 'Rhodora' testifies:

> In May, when sea-winds pierced our solitudes,
> I found the fresh Rhodora in the woods,
> Spreading its leafless blooms in a damp nook,
> To please the desert and the sluggish brook.
> The purple petals, fallen in the pool,
> Made the black water with their beauty gay;
> Here might the red-bird come his plumes to cool,
> And court the flower that cheapens his array.
> Rhodora! if the sages ask thee why
> This charm is wasted on the earth and sky,

25

Tell them, dear, that if eyes were made for seeing,
Then Beauty is its own excuse for being:
Why thou wert there, O rival of the rose!
I never thought to ask, I never knew;
But, in my simple ignorance, suppose
The self-same Power that brought me there brought
    you.[2]

Emerson is usually considered a more accomplished stylist than Sigourney or Oakes-Smith, who are cited in the introduction. But his lines are still lax and his language lazy. The excessive use of pronouns and function words (half the total) slows the rhythm down, giving a sluggish effect all too mimetic of the brook in question. Phrases like 'damp nook,' 'sluggish brook,' and 'the sages' are vague and clichéd. Finally, the speaker's pose of 'simple ignorance' is unconvincing. To this reader at any rate, the poem's conclusion is not only banal but unpleasantly coy.

Aside from the possibly surprising effect his metrical irregularity might have had on a nineteenth-century ear (less accustomed than our own to variation), there is nothing linguistically—or conceptually—refreshing in Emerson's poem. Although the poet purports to instruct his reader, he does not challenge him or her. On the contrary, by using language in a conventional manner, Emerson subverts whatever intention he had to make his reader 'see' something in a new way. We leave 'Rhodora' not in a state of wonder and surprise, but confirmed in our belief that beauty is beauty and God is everywhere.

How different, then, is the effect when Dickinson 'moralizes' on a flower:

The Dandelion's pallid tube
Astonishes the Grass,
And Winter instantly becomes
An infinite Alas—
The tube uplifts a signal Bud
And then a shouting Flower,—
The Proclamation of the Suns
That sepulture is o'er.[3]

(#1519, P,1048)

Whatever else she intended by it, Dickinson's use of language in this poem is designed to wake us up. Indeed, 'waking up' is what 'The Dandelion's pallid tube' is about. Playing on the traditional analogy between Christ's rising and the coming of spring, the poet identifies the flower's pale tube with the noisy trumpet (*tubus* akin to *tuba* trumpet) announcing the resurrection of the 'Suns' (and, inevitably, 'Son'). The bud is a 'signal Bud' because it is both single and a sign (of things to come, a natural *sema*). The head is a 'shouting Flower' because it is YELL-ow (a 'loud' color),[4] because it 'tells' loudly what the bud only signed, and because it is bell-shaped like the flared end of the (shouting) trumpet. '[S]epulture' refers to winter death and to Christ's rising from the tomb, the event which 'proclaimed' (*proclamare*, to cry out before) our resurrection even as antetype 'proclaims' (foreshadows) type. The much abused dandelion is, we discover, the very Christ of flowers—like that other cast-off symbol of Christ, Cordelia, 'most rich being poor,/Most choice forsaken, and most loved despised' (*King Lear*, I.i.250–1). Weed it may be, but we misprize it at our peril.

Dickinson's poem is a joke, a tease, wicked as the submerged eye-pun on yellow. Yet at the same time, it is wonderfully and wittily wise. With one quarter of Emerson's words, she conveys a statement considerably more complex than that proffered by the Concord sage.

She has made her flower at least as vivid. She has brought her language totally alive, drawing on its etymological roots as well as its surface meaning (one of her favorite linguistic strategies). Finally, she has written a poem that is inimitably hers. For while it requires sensitivity to see beauty in a hidden forest flower, it takes Emily Dickinson to turn a garden pest into the trumpet of the Lord. Even the seventeenth-century British 'metaphysicals,' from whom she may have taken this technique, could not best her at it.

To bring about these effects, Dickinson had to take risks—risks with her language and risks with her audience's willingness to play along. Reading her poem, we must think and see in new ways and entertain disruptions in wording, tone, subject and grammar for which conventional usage provides few if any precedents. In *Emily Dickinson: A Poet's Grammar*, Cristanne Miller analyzes the ways in which Dickinson's disjunctive play with language helps prepare the reader for the reordering of traditionally-received meaning that occurs within her texts. To Miller, disjunction (cleavages caused by grammatical separation or—I would add—by the posing of logically contradictory opposites) lies at the heart of Dickinson's technique and makes possible her unique vision and style. Dickinson uses disjunction, Miller writes, to reorder 'meaning along associative, analogical lines in order to express what was before inexpressible or unseen and out of a love of play with language.'[5] Viewed in this way—the way Dickinson uses it, for example, in 'The Dandelion's pallid tube'—disjunction is an integrative force.

But as the poet obliquely acknowledges in the '*Fee Bee*' passage quoted as an epigraph to this chapter, Dickinson's love of linguistic innovation had a darker side as well, and to some readers this side may seem closer to chaos than it does to play. One poem where Dickinson's use of disjunction obviously has this effect is 'Four Trees—upon a solitary/Acre.' In this poem, Dickinson deliberately exploits the ambiguities of grammatical disjunction in order to reflect the ambiguity of a world in which the existence of ordered meaning—of a logical relationship between events—cannot be known. Written twenty years before 'The Dandelion's pallid tube,' and the product, seemingly, of a very different sensibility, 'Four Trees' represents the furthest reach of Dickinson's agnostic metaphysics and the poetic *terminus ad quem* for her use of disjunction as a stylistic device:

Four Trees—upon a solitary
Acre—
Without Design
Or Order, or Apparent
+Action—
+Maintain—

The Sun—upon a Morning
meets them—
The Wind—
No Nearer Neighbor—have
they—
But God—

The Acre gives them—
Place—
They—Him—Attention of
Passer by—
Of Shadow, or of Squirrel,
haply—
Or Boy—

What Deed +is Their's
Unto the General Nature—
What Plan

They severally—+retard—or
further—
Unknown—

+signal—notice   +Do reign—
+they bear   +promote—or hinder—
                    (#742, F,903–4)

This is a poem without a period. It is also a poem without
a conclusion—in both senses of the term. The world
which it depicts (and mirrors through its own apparent
randomness and fragmentation), is a world of discrete
entities and seemingly accidental events. Each actor in
this little drama is stripped to its bare linguistic essence:
four trees, an acre, sun, wind, passer-by, squirrel, boy.
Nothing distinguishes them beyond their generic iden-
tity. They bear only a coincidental relationship to each
other, joined yet separated by Dickinson's ubiquitous
(and ambiguous) dash.

Dashes control the poem, breaking up its flow into dis-
crete, seemingly randomly-ordered parcels. They leave
the relationship between each unit grammatically in-
determinate so that, as Miller observes of Dickinson's
use of this strategy generally,[6] the poet is able to make
words function in more than one syntactical relation-
ship: 'Design' with both 'Trees' and 'Maintain,' 'Main-
tain' with 'Trees' and 'Sun,' 'Sun' with 'Maintain' and
'meets,' 'God' with both 'Neighbor' and 'Acre,' 'Place,'
with 'Acre' and 'They.' Such constructions read back and
forth, their exact meaning as impossible to pin down,
finally, as the meaning of the trees themselves. If there is
a 'Plan' to all this, and if this plan is furthered or retarded
by these trees, we will never know.

Where disjunction in 'The Dandelion's pallid tube'
complicates and enriches meaning, reordering it, as
Miller says, 'along associative, analogical lines,' the

disjunctions in 'Four Trees' break meaning down, fragmenting it into isolated and random units. There is, the poem's grammar seems to insist, 'no natural or divine plan of things keeping meaning safe from the threat of incipient chaos.'[7] There is no connection (beyond ambiguity) between events. The connections we assert are merely the order we artificially impose upon the void that God—or nature—deals us.

Not surprisingly, to critics sensitive to the potential for disintegration within disjunction—its basic lawlessness—Dickinson's predilection for this particular poetic strategy may seem less playful than it does threatening, despite her use of it in more affirmative moods. '[I]f poetry is to exist at all, it really must have form and grammar, and must rhyme when it professes to rhyme,' fulminates Andrew Lang, a late-nineteenth-century reviewer. 'The wisdom of the ages and the nature of man insist on so much.'[8] In what is in many ways an update of this view, David Porter declares:

> We have in Dickinson not order but restlessness. . . . Hers is an idiom that is hyperconscious, a relentless performing of the artistic consciousness in an unintelligible world. Irregular in observation, the idiom is autogenous, turned inward, decomposing the world into piecemeal reflexions and aggressive words.[9]

What to Miller is 'play of the mind' and 'profoundly creative experimentation,' to critics like Porter and Lang is willful disobedience and a rejection of intelligible, that is, well-ordered, speech.

Both viewpoints are correct, of course. Dickinson was creative and experimental. She had a tremendous capacity to play, a capacity that came to her early and, as the dating of 'The Dandelion's pallid tube' (c. 1881) testifies,

stayed with her to the end of her life. But by the time
Dickinson began writing poetry seriously in the late
1850s, her play had become earnest and at stake was not
just the language of poetry but the world view upon
which nineteenth-century poetics and metaphysics were
based. Put another way, the nineteenth-century review-
ers who, like Lang, rejected Dickinson when her poetry
first appeared were in some respects closer to the poet's
'truth' than those, like Higginson, who praised her 'deep
thought' while excusing her bad grammar.[10] Bad gram-
mar was only an aspect of Dickinson's rebellion but it
spoke to the deepest part of that rebellion—her willful
rejection of the laws upon which her culture was based
('the wisdom of the ages and the nature of man'). The
dark side of her poetic must never be minimized. In the
unconventionality of her grammar as in the unconven-
tionality of her thinking, Dickinson was striking at the
foundations supporting Western phallocentric thought.

In a series of poems beginning in the early 1860s,
Dickinson describes what might best be called her fall
from metaphysical grace and the epistemological impact
this event had upon her. In these poems, Dickinson's
confrontation with the abyss becomes the central meta-
phor for her vision of a world from which transcendent
meaning has been withdrawn and in which, therefore,
the speaker is free to reach any conclusion she wishes or,
indeed, to reach no conclusion at all.[11]

'I felt a Funeral, in my Brain,' c. 1862, is one such
poem. On the surface, this poem is about death or,
possibly, madness. But, finally, affectively, if it is 'about'
anything, it is about dread. In it, to use Miller's words,
Dickinson does not reorder 'what formerly appeared to

be conclusively known.'[12] She tells what it *feels like* to
realize that nothing can be known at all:

I felt a Funeral, in my Brain,
And Mourners to and fro
Kept treading—treading—till
it seemed
That Sense was breaking through—

And when they all were seated,
A Service, like a Drum—
Kept beating—beating—till
I thought
My Mind was going numb—

And then I heard them
lift a Box
And creak across my ~~Brain~~
Soul
With those same Boots of
Lead, again,
Then Space—began to toll,

As all the Heavens were
a Bell,
And Being, but an Ear,
And I, and Silence, some
strange Race
Wrecked, solitary, here—

And then, a Plank in
Reason, broke,
And I dropped down, and
down—
And hit a World, at every
+plunge,
And +Finished knowing—then—

Crash—+Got through—

(#280, F,341–42)

As in the surrealist paintings of de Chirico and Magritte, outsize 'humanistic' detail functions in this poem to evoke all the terror that the isolated individual feels when confronting nothingness—the abyss. In the poem's otherwise emptied-out landscape, 'the Heavens' become a 'Bell,' 'Being' an 'Ear.' Whether it is death or insanity that opens up this vision to her, what the speaker realizes is that she is utterly alone and totally free. There is neither a sustaining God nor a sustaining scaffold of meaning to support her. Like the trapdoor on a gallows or like the planks supporting a coffin until it is dropped into the grave, the 'bottom' drops out of reality. For the speaker, anything is possible in a world that is fundamentally absurd—where you can drop 'down, and down' and 'hit a World, at every plunge.' As in 'Four Trees,' the only conclusion to this experience is the conclusion that not-knowing (not just death but the acceptance of ignorance) brings.

In a second poem, 'I never hear that one is dead,' *c.* 1874, Dickinson treats her confrontation with the abyss in somewhat more explicit (and considerably less melodramatic) terms. In this poem, the speaker's isolation is attributed directly to the fact that she is willing to face what others will not admit—the irrationality or absurdity of their belief, the nothingness that gapes not only outside the self but within:

> I never hear that one is dead
> Without the chance of Life
> Afresh annihilating me
> That mightiest Belief,
>
> Too mighty for the Daily mind
> That tilling it's abyss,
> Had Madness, had it once or twice
> The yawning Consciousness,

Beliefs are Bandaged, like the Tongue
When Terror were it told
In any Tone commensurate
Would strike us instant Dead

I do not know the man so bold
He dare in lonely Place
That awful stranger Consciousness
Deliberately face—

1. that one is dead] that one has died—
8. yawning Consciousness] consciousness of this.
14. lonely Place] lonesome Place/ secret Place
16] look squarely in the Face.

(#1323, P,915)

Contemplating death or possibly madness, the speaker in this poem discovers in her self a capacity for doubt that terrifies her. The absurdity and random quality of death, like the absurdity and random quality of madness—both of which Dickinson summarizes as 'the chance of life'— annihilates belief. Whatever 'the Daily mind' (that is, the conventional mind) may wish to think, the speaker knows that the only meaning life has is the meaning she chooses to give it. Indeed, it is precisely this knowledge that strikes terror into her soul but which she feels must be 'told' (and 'tolled') anyway.

Isolated by her experience of the abyss, Dickinson's speaker is also isolated by her conscious knowledge of it, a knowledge which, she declares, others refuse to share. Unlike herself, they will not look into the nothingness that yawns at their feet. Their thoughts are 'bandaged,' and ironically, though they speak together, their tongues (like the clappers of so many bells) are bandaged too. Only the speaker is determined to say what she knows—that the solid world we live in, like the planks beneath our feet, is a lie.[13] Whether pain, death, or madness makes us aware of it, the abyss stretches out before us. The only way across it, as Dickinson explains in a brief poem, written *c.* 1862, is to move blindly, as if one were in a trance:

There is a pain—so utter—
It swallows +substance up—
Then covers the Abyss with Trance—
So memory can step
Around—across—upon it—
As one within a Swoon—
Goes +safely—where an Open Eye—
Would drop Him—Bone by Bone.

+Being
+steady—
+spill Him—

(#599, F,544)

When read together, these poems suggest that by the early 1860s, Dickinson knew that she had passed beyond the safe limits of nineteenth-century American thought. As she put it with succinct brilliance in 'I saw no Way— The /Heavens were stitched,' (*c.* 1862), she had gone 'Beyond the Dip of Bell.' The primary reference is to harbor buoy-bells, not to church bells, as it is sometimes glossed. It did not matter whether the 'Funeral' inside her brain was for the death of 'God' or for the death of 'Reason,' or simply for the death of her own 'substance' or 'Being,' devoured by pain or by some other cause. The experience had opened up a knowledge of nothingness which, to quote Donne, 'calls all in doubt'—not just Christian eschatology but Emerson's optimistic transcendentalism as well. As fixed poles for metaphysics— *transcendent* means by which to discover direction and meaning—'The Heavens' and 'The Earth' (God and nature) were shut. The speaker had only herself to rely on in a universe whose meaning, if any, she could not grasp:

I saw no Way—The
Heavens were stitched—
I felt the Columns close—
The Earth reversed her
Hemispheres—
I touched the Universe—

And back it slid—
and I alone—
A Speck upon a Ball—
Went out upon Circum-
ference—
Beyond the Dip of Bell—

(#378, F,738)

Like a giant clockwork mechanism, the universe in this
poem slides back on itself, leaving Dickinson's speaker
utterly exposed and, at the same time, completely closed
out. Both the singularity of her situation—'A Speck upon
a Ball'—and the correspondingly cosmic dimensions of
her quest are revealed. In a world where God is hidden
and the earth shut, the individual must make what
meaning she can out of the emptiness surrounding her.
The past, together with its metaphysical positions, no
longer provides a safe harbor. Like Melville's Ishmael,
she clings to her plank (her coffin?), alone and at sea.

In 'I saw no Way,' Dickinson stresses her enormous
sense of isolation. But this poem also suggests that by
1862, its presumed date of composition, the poet realized
how dangerous her quest was and how fragile the 'plank
in/ Reason' that prevented her from becoming utterly
lost. In 'A single Clover Plank,' c. 1875, the speaker
describes with deceptive playfulness the fate that awaits
her should she completely lose her grip on the possibility
of a rational order and drop into the surrounding abyss.
Ostensibly about a bumblebee, 'A single Clover Plank' is

a recasting of the speaker's situation in 'I saw no Way.' In spite of its surface lightness, however, it is in some respects a far darker poem.

A single Clover Plank
Was all that saved a Bee
A Bee I personally knew
From sinking in the sky—

Twixt Firmament above
And Firmament below
The Billows of Circumference
Were sweeping him away—

The idly swaying Plank
Responsible to nought
A sudden Freight of Wind assumed
And Bumble Bee was not—

This harrowing event
Transpiring in the Grass
Did not so much as wring from him
A wandering "Alas"—

  1. Clover Plank] Clover Spar
  2. Was all that saved] Alone sustained—/ [Alone] upheld—
  4] In crisis in the sky—/ in Hazard [in the sky]
  11] A sudden Freight of Wind took on—

(#1343, P,927–8)

Beneath its whimsical narrative, this poem duplicates the situation and spatial conditions of 'I saw no Way.' In both poems, the protagonist is 'A Speck upon a Ball,' caught between 'Firmament above/And Firmament below,' that is, between heaven and earth. In both, she or he goes 'out upon Circumference,' equated by means of submerged metaphor with an ocean (presumably, the ocean of doubt). Thus, in 'I saw no Way—,' Dickinson speaks of 'the Dip of Bell'; in 'A single Clover Plank,' she refers to 'Spar,' 'sinking,' and 'Billows.' Only the fates of the two protagonists differ. In the earlier poem, the speaker's fate is unclear. She may survive the experience of going out to sea. Then again, she may not. In 'A single Clover Plank,' there is no doubt: 'Bumble Bee was not' (not/nought/nothing). For bumblebees, at least, the experience was fatal.

And for poets?

In *Dickinson: The Modern Idiom*, David Porter analyzes the qualities of Dickinson's writing which he believes lead toward what he calls 'terminal modernism.' As much a victim as a beneficiary of her enormous linguistic gifts, Dickinson, he argues, had no poetic 'program,' nor any real comprehension of what she was about. Her poems are linguistic enactments in a meaningless void. '[D]isinherited from transcendent knowledge' (that is, presumably, from the 'wisdom of the ages'), they are 'autogenous' and discrete.[14] They are the crisis itself.

As we have seen, a poem like 'Four Trees' seems to support Porter's argument. In it, the fragmentation of meaning is complete. Not only does the poem deny the possibility of transcendence, it queries the possibility of any kind of significance whatsoever, even the significance of discrete words. But any attempt to assess Dickinson's poetic must weigh this poem against poems like 'The Dandelion's pallid tube,' in which Dickinson employs disjunction to reorder meaning rather than to break it down. And this assessment must also account for the fact that Dickinson clearly *did* understand the metaphysical and linguistic risks she was taking.

While Dickinson's insouciant bumblebee may experience his absorption into nothingness randomly and without comprehension, Dickinson herself was hardly so blind. On the contrary, the variants in 'A single Clover Plank' indicate that she fully recognized the 'hazard [in the sky]' that is, the gamble as well as the danger inherent in her metaphysics. More than that, she was consciously prepared to take the risk. As an adolescent, Dickinson told Abiah Root that she was determined 'to buffet the sea,' because she 'love[d] the danger.' The 'shore' (that is, the security offered by a conventional life and conventional thought) might be safer, but, she told her friend, she preferred to let her 'fancies'—that is, her rebellious thoughts as well as her poetry—bloom (L,104).

In maturity, Dickinson was no less bold and no less determined to act this 'program' out. Her doom might prove as 'harrowing' as that of her beloved bee; but such a fate was still preferable to the security of a 'tied-up' tongue and 'bandaged' beliefs. Exquisitely sensitive to the latent existentialist tensions in nineteenth-century thought—tensions that would one day surface in post-modern travail—Dickinson took her chances. As she said in 'These tested Our Horizon,' heaven and immortality were, in any case, 'A Dice—a Doubt—' (#886, F,1068). Like Melville, who took the same gamble, she had as much to gain as lose, by challenging her period's metaphysics.

'In a Life that stopped guessing, you and I should not feel at home,' Dickinson wrote to Susan Gilbert Dickinson c. 1878 (L,632). Even more bluntly, she declared to the same correspondent c. 1884, 'Faith is *Doubt*' (L,830). 'Search,' she declared in a prose fragment on the power of the imagination, 'surpasses the occupying . . . estimation' (L,922). These were the principles by which she lived. They were not principles designed to ensure one's sense of stability or security. Our current crisis in philosophical thought testifies to that. But then again, neither were they necessarily counsels of chaos, meaninglessness and despair. Their essence lay in the poet's determination to maintain her intellectual freedom—her capacity to question prevailing beliefs, 'the wisdom of the ages,' 'transcendent knowledge', 'the nature of man'—whatever cost or 'crisis' she might incur.

Their consequence is to be found not only in the poet's philosophical risk-taking, but in her risk-taking poetics. Indeed, the latter are in many ways the inevitable result of the former, the praxis to which her life of 'guessing' inevitably led.

Isolated by her confrontation with the abyss, Dickinson was also freed by it. By the early 1860s, her need to pass 'Beyond the Dip of Bell,' that is, beyond conventional limits, can be seen in every aspect of her work. Using the hymnal stanza as the basic frame within which she wrote (rather as she used Christianity to supply the framework within which she questioned), she handles the givens of her genre with an unconventionality so great that we are still struggling today to grasp the full extent of her radicalism.

In her poetry as in her thought, Dickinson became an original, a being who was self-conceived and therefore always capable of change.[15] Work done on the manuscript versions of her poetry by Susan Howe, in particular, suggests that no aspect of her writing can ever be completely stabilized—not the subjects on which she appears to write or the forms her poems take.[16] (This applies not only to matters such as spelling, syntax, grammatical forms, punctuation, meter and rhyme but also to variants, line length, spacing and stanza break.) All these aspects of Dickinson's poetry are continually shifting from poem to poem and from version to version of the same poem. Whether as editors or readers, we cannot pin her down. No poet was ever more fluid.

41

The sizeable number of poems that Dickinson left in semi-final or working draft after 1860 suggests that the very act of finishing or perfecting a poem (writing it down in what we call 'fair copy') became repugnant to her. Poems were not fixed, any more than life or thought were. They were process, discovery, tentative and delicate 'planks,' by which, in one poem, she makes her 'slow and cautious / way' (#875, F,1060) or, as in another, 'pearly strands' she weaves each night 'from Nought to Nought—/In unsubstantial Trade' (#605, H283d). She would not—or could not—finish them.

In some poems, Dickinson appears to leave her alternate readings simply as that: traces of the poetic process. Like the dashes with which so many of her poems conclude, they are evidence of the impossibility of final choice, of definitive endings. In others, however, these variants (which are effectively another form of disjunction in Dickinson's poetry), are inextricable from the substance of the poem itself. The use of both 'crisis' and 'hazard' in 'A single Clover Plank' is an example.

In 'The Spider holds a Silver Ball,' a poem which, like 'A single Clover Plank,' Dickinson presumably left in semi-final draft, the multiple variants are, it can be argued, what the poem is about. As a result of her refusal to choose among them, Dickinson is able to juxtapose two antithetical views of the spider-artist's (and her own) labors. As readers, we are forced to hold both views simultaneously in mind since, unselected by Dickinson, her variants must have equal authorial status in our eyes:

> The Spider holds a Silver Ball
> In unperceived Hands—
> +as He knits
> And +dancing softly +to Himself
> His +Yarn of Pearl—+unwinds—
> +expends—

He plies from Nought to Nought—
In unsubstantial Trade—
Supplants our Tapestries with His—
In half the period—

An Hour to rear supreme
His +Continents of Light—
Then +dangle from the Housewife's
Broom
His +Boundaries—forgot—

+Pursues his pearly strands—   +Coil—
+Theories   +perish by   +Sophistries
                    (#605, H283d)

In *The Madwoman in the Attic*, Gilbert and Gubar analyze this poem using Johnson's version of the text. On the basis of his edition, they argue that the poem is about Dickinson's situation as a private woman poet. Although she knows how valuable her artistic endeavors are, like the spider, she works in secret: 'mental pirouettes silently performed in the attic of Nobodaddy's house.' When she dies, 'unsympathetic male editors and female heirs' may sweep her efforts away.[17]

But this interpretation of the poem works only if we ignore the alternatives available in the manuscript version. In the manuscript, the spider constructs 'Continents' or 'Theories of Light.' He forgets 'Boundaries' or 'Sophistries.' While 'Continents' and 'Boundaries' harmonize with the Gilbert and Gubar interpretation (these are the variants that, following Johnson, they accept), 'Theories' and 'Sophistries' do not. The negative connotations of these words are inescapable and yield an entirely different reading of the text. The pragmatic housewife with her broom is not the only one to question the value of the spider's silver web. The speaker has her doubts too. For the worlds of light which the spider-artist

43

weaves both are and are not real. Insofar as they are art, they are the products of imagination; hence, they are insubstantial. Indeed, they are sophistries or lies. 'Now my dear friend,' Dickinson declared to Abiah Root in 1850, at the conclusion of a particularly florid passage of writing, 'let me tell you that these last thoughts are fictions. . . . They are flowers of speech, they both *make* and *tell* deliberate falsehoods, avoid them as the snake. . . .' (L,88).

Although Dickinson continued to indulge her taste for lies throughout her life (Ned, she wrote Mrs Holland in 1866, 'inherits his Uncle Emily's ardor for the lie' L,449), she never lost sight of the fact that on one level at least this is what her poems were. And it is this conflict, a conflict between two points of view, which 'The Spider holds a Silver Ball' asserts through its variants. By leaving both of her alternatives standing, Dickinson has refused to choose between two traditional conceptions of the poetic process. Like the debate in *A Midsummer Night's Dream* between Hippolyta and Theseus regarding the reliability of the lovers' narrative, the question which this poem raises is left unresolved. The poet may body forth the forms of things unknown ('Continents of Light') or he or she may turn a bush into a bear ('Sophistries' or lies).

How then are we to evaluate such art? What are we to make of the fact that it can be so easily swept away? That it is 'unsubstantial,' that it 'plies from Nought to Nought'? (Note the linguistic and situational echoes to 'A single Clover Plank.') Is the poet who is 'free' (who writes at night, whose work is never seen) a true maker or is she merely spinning away her substance and her time? Is there anything substantial (metaphysically as well as materially) to the Theories/Continents she creates?

These are the questions (and conflicts) that the poem

44

raises through its disjunctive variants and, *equally import-ant*, refuses to resolve. No choice is made between alternatives either on a formal or an epistemological level any more than Shakespeare indicates his choice in *Midsummer Night's Dream*. Formally, ontologically and epistemologically, the poem is left in doubt. We make of it what we will.

Had Dickinson been forced by the requirements of publication—or logic—to decide between her alternatives (between 'Continents' and 'Theories,' 'Boundaries' and 'Sophistries'), the meaning of the poem would have been radically diminished, as indeed it is diminished in current published versions. Dickinson could not 'finish' this poem because being unfinished—being left in doubt—is what it is about. To have made choices among its variants would have fixed it in time and space, giving it a resolution and permanency that would have been the greatest lie of all. For the conflict that Dickinson describes in this poem can never be resolved. It is fundamental to the paradox we call art.

Like the use of disjunction generally in Dickinson, the variants of 'The Spider holds a Silver Ball' force us to confront inherent contradictions within our human condition, contradictions which under normal circumstances we resist having to acknowledge. In such cases we see 'truth,' but by a very different slant, the slant produced by Dickinson's 'Compound Vision,' that is, by her extraordinary capacity to comprehend the duplicity of all things that simultaneously are and are not in a timebound world: 'Light—enabling Light—/The Finite—furnished/With the Infinite—' (#906, F,987).

For Dickinson, it was a matter of perspective and this perspective was one which accepted a priori that life was not an either/or proposition. Finally, it was both/and, that is, finite and infinite, existing and not existing, at once:

All overgrown by cunning moss,
All interspersed with weed,
The little cage of "Currer Bell"
In quiet "Haworth" laid.

This Bird—observing others
When frosts too sharp became
Retire to other latitudes—
Quietly did the same—

But differed in returning—
Since Yorkshire hills are green—
Yet not in all the nests I meet—
Can Nightingale be seen—
                    Or—
Gathered from many wanderings—
Gethsemane can tell
Thro' what transporting anguish
She reached the Asphodel!

Soft fall the sounds of Eden
Upon her puzzled ear—
Oh what an afternoon for
Heaven,
When "Bronte" entered there!

(#148, F,112–13)

Dickinson does not reject the possibility of life-after-death in this poem, she simply points out that there are other ways to speak about death—and one involves irreparable loss. We may feel more sympathy with the first version of this poem (stanzas one through three) or the second (stanzas one, four and five) or we may waver between alternatives as she does here. The one thing we cannot do after reading this poem *as she left it* is deny that two very different points of view exist. It is to Johnson's credit in the variorum edition that he suggests this may have been Dickinson's intention in leaving the poem as she did. And it is a sad commentary on the pressures of publication that in the single volume edition of her poetry, he leaves stanzas two and three out (thus creating, in effect, a poem Dickinson never wrote). 'All overgrown by cunning moss' is complete, is 'finished,' is itself, only if both its variants (both its ways of looking at death) are included.

Speaking of the variants in 'My Life had stood—a Loaded Gun,' Cristanne Miller declares:

> Dickinson's textual variants provide evidence that her poems originated as processes of thought based on the play of cumulative possibilities of meaning. More strongly even than the ambiguities of compression and syntax, variants contribute to the multiplicity of a text by requiring the reader's participation in establishing the text of a poem. . . . In poems with multiple word choice the reader must continuously stabilize the text by choosing what belongs in it and at the same time repeatedly return to account for the other, unchosen, possibilities of the poem's meaning.[18]

Writing to the sculptor Daniel Chester French to congratulate him on the unveiling of his statue of John Harvard, Dickinson put the same set of ideas more succinctly and with less caution. 'Success is dust,' she declares, 'but an aim forever touched with dew' (L,822).

It is in the aim that possibility lies and in the process that we discover meaning. What is finished is also what is dead ('dust'). While choosing among alternatives and stabilizing the poetic text might seem desirable strategies when reading or editing any other writer, this sort of stabilization can only kill Dickinson. To bring her to life we must, as Miller recommends, go back continuously to account for the other possibilities. Indeed, we must hold each poem's possibilities simultaneously in mind, for they are part of the poem's substance and cannot be separated from it. '"It is finished" can never be said of us,' Dickinson informed Mrs Holland in 1878 (L,613). She was speaking of immortality but the statement also applies to her art. Being unfinishable was the poetic 'program,' to use Porter's term, she enacted in all her work. As later chapters will make clear, to Dickinson this program best reflected the state of human knowledge and, perhaps, the human condition. Certainly, it was the program best suited to a woman poet trying to understand the world and her own condition free from the shibboleths (the 'bandages') of the past.

It is no wonder then that Dickinson rejected the fixities of the old grammar or that, as a result, critics committed to 'the wisdom of the ages' and 'the nature of man' reject her. Like our metaphysics, our grammar, even our spelling, presupposes the validity and rightful permanence of certain shared cultural beliefs. These beliefs guide us in our daily lives and organize our perceptions of the world, fixing it in certain ways. There is one sun, not many. A flower does not shout. A verb cannot function simultaneously in two separate and independent syntactical arrangements. Something cannot be and not be at the same time. Dickinson violates all these rules and others like them not once but over and over again in countless major and minor ways. Her poetry is anomic from beginning to end, a ceaseless attack on the basic laws of Aristotelean logic and (as a number of nineteenth-century reviewers observe) on what we think of fondly as the principles of common sense. The end result is that her poetry is constantly in flux, a restless, ever-changing medium, suited to her radically questioning, often violently anti-traditional, anti-masculinist, needs.

Had Higginson been more encouraging when Dickinson made her initial approach regarding publication, it is possible that Dickinson might have tried harder to accommodate nineteenth-century literary standards, but I doubt it. By the early 1860s, the sentimentality which characterizes much of her earliest writing had received a jolt from which it would never recover, and her own linguistic genius was fully revealed. She knew exactly what she had to offer. What she had to offer would not and could not be squared with public taste, whichever gender she belonged to.

But publishing itself had, finally, become antithetical to Dickinson's purpose and poetic. It was not just that most of her writing was too unconventional to pass muster. Equally important, the very act of publishing would have given her poems an ontological status she did not want them to have. Even recopying them for the 'fascicles,' as her small manuscript books are called, seems to have become oppressive to her. By the mid-1870s, she stopped trying to organize her poetry altogether. As often as not, poems written after that date are left as she first conceived them—on the odd scraps of paper she used to jot them down.[19]

But the result of this 'process poetic'—this refusal to finish—is not chaos. The result is poems of unique linguistic power that are free to explore ideas for which nineteenth-century American ideology, grammar and spelling made little if any room. In the chapters that follow I will trace some of Dickinson's explorations as they affect her poetry on religion, nature, psychological states and on female sexuality. That many of these poems exhibit the same kind of logical oppositions or disjunctions and the same kind of indeterminacy that characterize her grammar and her handling of her variants hardly needs saying. But they are not fragments set loose to jostle one another in a void. They are the purposeful—if often disturbing—work of a highly self-conscious creator, a creator who as a thinker and as a woman knew herself to stand outside the traditions, order and values of the phallocentric culture in which she lived.

Chapter Two

Pugilist and Poet

Audacity of Bliss, said Jacob to the Angel "I will not let thee go except I bless thee"—Pugilist and Poet, Jacob was correct—

(Dickinson to T. W. Higginson, 1886)

No poetry by Dickinson evinces more clearly her need to test alternative points of view than the poetry she wrote on religious themes. Like other major writers of her era, Dickinson was intensely, almost obsessively, concerned with ultimate questions: the nature of God, death, immortality. And like a number of these writers— Emerson, Hawthorne, Melville—she tends to locate these concerns in the isolated individual's quest for understanding. But our ability to track the course of Dickinson's spiritual development is profoundly affected by the nature of her medium, the personal lyric, and by the diverse way she handled this form. Indeed, given that Dickinson voices statements of faith and of doubt both early and late in her career, it is difficult to know whether 'development' as such occurred at all, let alone to systematize the conclusions (if any) that she drew.[1] After hearing a sermon on predestination, Dickinson remarked that she did not 'respect "doctrines"' (L,346). And she was deeply suspicious of those who promulgated them—even, perhaps especially, when they wore the cloth, and even when they seemed to assume positions with which she herself would agree:

> He preached upon "Breadth" till it argued him narrow—
> The Broad are too broad to define
> And of "Truth" until it proclaimed him a Liar—
> The Truth never flaunted a Sign—
>
> Simplicity fled from his counterfeit presence
> As Gold the Pyrites would shun—
> What confusion would cover the innocent Jesus
> To meet so enabled a Man!
>
> (#1207, P,839)

As David Reynolds observes of this poem, in it Dickinson uses 'the tools of antebellum imaginative preaching—paradox, humor, startling metaphor, stress upon the human Jesus—to undermine preaching itself.'[2] Even the broadest approach to religious doctrine will argue itself both narrow and a lie, once it mounts the pulpit to proclaim its "Truth." Reared in an era when theological points were the subject of vituperative debate in the popular press, and surrounded by religious revivalism and sectarian controversy, Dickinson, as she said regarding the sermon on predestination, chose not to 'listen.' Rather than achieving answers, her own religious quest became a posing of positions, positions which allowed her to undermine one possibility by reference to another, not infrequently subverting both. This chapter will

examine some of the 'positions' Dickinson took, espe-
cially as these positions reflect the poet's sensitivity to the
issues raised by the 'feminization' of religion (to use Ann
Douglas's term) occurring in her day. While Dickinson
was fully aware of the inadequacies of sentimentalized
religion, its influence on her, especially in its implicit
critique of the Puritan conception of a sovereign God,
was more profound than has been generally realized and
may well account for why she felt justified in engaging in
pitched battle with this Calvinist notion of deity through-
out her life.[3]

One of the most striking features of nineteenth-century
American Protestantism is the rise within it of a feminized
or, better, domesticized concept of God. Ann Douglas has
traced this rise at length in *The Feminization of American
Culture*. Suffice it to say here, that it represented a repudi-
ation on the part of many women *and* men of the doctrine
of a sovereign God fundamental to New England Puritan-
ism. In particular, it represented the need of many be-
lievers to develop a concept of God more ethically
compatible with the democratic and commercial values
dominating nineteenth-century America than the Puritan
deity could be.[4]

Employing a gubernatorial model, New England Pur-
itans had refused to limit God's power in any way. As
much the product of their authoritarian political ideals as
of their commitment to the Calvinist doctrine of predes-
tination, their God was a sublime, unalterable Other, a
transcendent Being, who neither could nor should be
comprehended in human ethical terms. God, Samuel
Willard declared, 'acts as a great Monarch, who gives not
an account of His matters to the Children of Men, but

holds the Creature in full Subordination to his absolute pleasure.'[5] In his famous sermon, 'Sinners in the Hands of an Angry God,' Jonathan Edwards defines God's 'pleasure' as 'his arbitrary will, restrained by no obligation, hindered by no manner of difficulty.'[6] To Edwards, as to other Puritans, this will was capable of enacting whatever it wished. It saved or damned whom it chose, by its mercy alone. Nothing man did in his own right could alter it.

Rigorous and tough-minded, Puritans were fully prepared to accept the consequences of refusing to limit God's power in this way. As Richard Forrer has observed in his study of theodicean conflicts in the nineteenth century, the Puritan conception of God's sovereignty became inevitably, therefore, a defense of the presence of evil in the world. However great their vision of God's beauty, majesty and love, men like Edwards were also prepared to accept that evil was part of His redemptive plan. '[I]t is necessary,' Edwards declares:

> that God's awful majesty, his authority and dreadful greatness, justice, and holiness, should be manifested. But this could not be, unless sin and punishment had been decreed. . . . And as it is necessary that there should be evil, because the display of the glory of God could not but be imperfect and incomplete without it, so evil is necessary, in order to the highest happiness of the creature, and the completeness of that communication of God, for which he made the world; because the creature's happiness consists in the knowledge of God, and sense of his love.[7]

Secure in their own covenant of grace, by which God had, presumably, elected them to be His chosen people, founding His city in the Wilderness, the Puritans were ready, in effect, to accept the damnation of the greater part of mankind if that was necessary for the fulfillment of God's purposes on earth and our knowledge of His love.

As Forrer observes, the argument which Edwards makes 'for morality could have little appeal to those outside the select religious coterie of the already saved, since, in this view, no moral striving can contribute to one's salvation until God, according to His own good pleasure, infuses it with His grace.'[8] To the Puritans, who believed themselves so elected, covenant theology provided a closed system that was morally satisfactory. But in the post-revolutionary era, its appropriateness to the changing conditions of a developing democracy was increasingly challenged—as was the notion of a deity who could act in such a totally arbitrary way.

In the second half of the eighteenth century, rationalist theologians attacked the Puritan image of God as elitist and unethical. In the century that followed, these same objections provided the foundation for a new concept of God, one as Douglas demonstrates, cast in a 'fundamentally maternal and affective' model.[9] 'God,' the Methodist theologian, R. S. Foster, writes, 'is a sovereign God not a sovereign devil. He is not an irresponsible, blind, capricious, sovereignty, His rights and His rule are not resolvable into mere arbitrary acts of will.'[10] In the same vein, William Channing argues that 'were a human parent to form himself on the Universal Father, as described by Calvinism . . . we should charge him with a cruelty not surpassed in the annals of the world.'[11] Instead, Channing offers a God who is 'an all-communicating Parent . . . who has sympathies with us as kindred beings . . . who looks on us with parental interest, and whose great design it is to communicate to us for ever, and in freer and fuller streams, his own power, goodness, and joy.'[12] And it is this God, a God reshaped to conform to the more liberal attitudes of an enlightened

55

political era, that provided the basis for the domesticized notion of deity that pervades nineteenth-century sentimental literature, in particular, the literature written by women.

If nineteenth-century American women poets were the ideological propagandists of their period—the purveyors of 'warm domestic affection, and pure religious feeling'—a 'parental' conception of God was their principal stock-in-trade, the solution they offered to all life's cares. Bearing only vestigial reminders of the Puritans' majestic and forbidding presence, God became our loving father instead—a father who taught by example and guided with tender care. No matter what storms beset humanity, God was there, His promise of salvation the one hope in which mankind could put full trust. '"There shall be light"' Elizabeth J. Eames confidently asserts in a poem listing at length the various ills to which flesh is heir:

Onward and upward, O my soul!
    Let they endeavour be—
Though dark the cloud-mist 'bove thee roll,
    Light shall be given to thee;
Though stormiest waves and billows rock
    Thy human bark at will,
Thou shalt have strength to bear the shock—
    Be Hope thy anchor still.

(May 255)

Even the most aching questions of human life, those most likely to make us aware of the arbitrariness of God's judgments and the reality of evil—the death of the young and the innocent, for example—found their answer in a 'kindly' father above. At least so Eliza Follen claims to believe in 'On the Death of a Beautiful Young Girl':

The young, the lovely pass away,
Ne'er to be seen again;
Earth's fairest flowers too soon decay;
Its blasted trees remain.

Full oft we see the brightest thing
That lifts its head on high,
Smile in the light, then droop its wing,
And fade away, and die.

And kindly is the lesson given,
Then dry the falling tear;
They came to raise our hearts to heaven,
They go to call us there.

(May 169)

In poems such as this (and the many like it) not only has God been fully exonerated for the misfortunes besetting humanity, but Heaven has become the recompense for every ill. Indeed, 'Heaven' has become the answer to all the problems posed by human misery—in effect, an anesthetic to pain. And it was as an anesthetic that these poets (like sentimentalists generally in this movement) used it. Never, perhaps, in the history of Christianity was the promise of life-after-death employed so cavalierly or so popularly to deny the reality of pain, the intractable Being-ness of suffering, evil and loss, and never, as a result, had so many people felt assured that they too would make it into heaven.

'The old Calvinist way of church,' Ann Douglas writes, 'assumed, and expected, pain: not the passive suffering of deprivation and martyrdom, but the active distress of assault and achievement.'[13] Pain led the afflicted soul to an awareness of sin. But to nineteenth-century sentimentalists, pain was something you escaped from in feeling (the hope of heaven, the love of God). Even the death of a beautiful young girl was a

57

'kindly' lesson, turning our thoughts to a better life. Real loss, like real evil, was denied. Heaven had become a democracy where all could enter if they only believed (or felt) enough.[14]

There was no way that Emily Dickinson, as a mid-nineteenth-century woman, could escape this kind of sentimentality. As Douglas and others have shown, sentimentalism was the language middle-class women spoke, the point of view they absorbed, the way they thought; and Dickinson was one of them. Its influence can be seen in her youthfully effusive letters to Susan Gilbert and other women friends and in her early attraction to authors such as Longfellow and 'Ik Marvel' (Donald K. Mitchell). It can also be seen in the religious concerns her early poetry, in particular, expresses. Like the infamous Emmeline Grangerford, the nineteenth-century's 'archetypal' woman poet, the young Emily Dickinson was obsessed with death and like many of her compatriots she, too, seems to have fantasized a domesticated heaven. Indeed, although she hardly cites American women poets by name, there are times, particularly in her early poetry, when she can sound remarkably like them, as in 'A poor—torn Heart—a tattered heart' (c. 1859), for instance:

> The Angels, happening that way
> This dusty heart espied—
> Tenderly took it up from toil,
> And carried it to God—
> There—Sandals for the Barefoot—
> There—gathered from the gales
> Do the blue Havens by the hand
> Lead the wandering sails.
>
> (#78, P. 63. Version to Sue.)

Since Dickinson accompanied the version of this poem

which she sent to Sue with an illustration of angels carrying little Nell to heaven, clipped from her father's copy of *The Old Curiosity Shop*, she may have been having fun with it. When taken together, the poem and the picture seem excessive. But even if this is true, the poem itself remains staunchly within the sentimental tradition. Right down to the muddled metaphors in its concluding lines, it contains all the basic ingredients Douglas describes: the same domestication of God and death, the same view of heaven as a recompense for human suffering, the same refusal to admit a clear demarcation between life and death, the same need to concretize heaven's details, here, minimally, the sandals for bare feet.[15] If nothing else, this poem, and others like it ('Taken from men—this morning' [#53] and 'Going to Heaven!' [#79], for example) confirm Dickinson's religious links to her period. Not only was she familiar with sentimentalized religious notions, but she was ready to reflect them back. Whether taken seriously or for purposes of parody, the sentimentalists' concept of life-after-death and their view of death as a transition to a better life were Dickinson's starting points as well.

But it is also clear that even early on, Dickinson was restless with many aspects of sentimental thinking. Thus, for example, she accompanied a batch of novels sent to Susan Gilbert in 1852 with a note declaring that, though 'sweet and true,' and sure to 'do one good,' these stories about 'pure little lives, loving God and their parents' did not '*bewitch* [her] any' (L,195). And she uses the same deadly adjective to characterize a long lugubrious poem on the death of a child which she sent to Mary Warner four years later. '[T]he verses,' she writes Warner, are 'very sweet' and 'I'm sure that you will love them' (L,326). Although she evidently considered such 'sweetness' appropriate for her friends, her own attitude toward it, to judge by her choice of qualifiers, was ambivalent at best.

By the time Dickinson reached maturity, she was no longer able to suppress her distaste. As we shall see, sentimentalism was in many ways a positive force in Dickinson's work, especially in her nature poetry, but its view of God left too many questions unanswered, too many anomalies unresolved. Because of its very seamlessness—the ease with which it offered up God's love and the hope of heaven as answers to every ill—it required resistance. Like the little boy in 'The Emperor's New Clothes,' the poet was prepared to point her finger at what 'the Daily mind' refused to admit: the horrible contradictions marring God's 'love,' the foolishness and dishonesty of a naive ('pure little') faith. In a c. 1862 poem written on the knife-edge of irony, she problematizes the sentimentalists' easy belief:

Glee—The great storm is over—
Four—have recovered the Land—
Forty—gone down together—
Into the boiling Sand—

Ring—for the Scant Salvation—
Toll—for the bonnie Souls—
Neighbor—and friend—and Bridegroom—
Spinning upon the Shoals—

How they will tell the Story—
When Winter shake the Door—
Till the Children urge— +ask—
But the Forty—
Did they—Come back no more?

Then a softness[2]—suffuse the Story—
And a silence[1]—the Teller's Eye—
And the Children—no further
question—
And only the Sea—reply—

(#619, F,766)

At first glance, 'Glee—The great storm is over' looks like a relatively transparent celebration of God's miraculous mercy—and it was probably read this way when first published in 1890. In fact, however, it is a highly subversive attack on precisely that kind of thinking. With an extraordinary economy of means, Dickinson has employed the basic elements of genre painting in order to expose the deceitfulness upon which sentimentalism (whether in art or religion) depends. The warm little cottage (snow-covered, perhaps), the inspired teller, the circle of listening children, the boiling sand outside the door are the all-too-familiar ingredients of a specific kind of aesthetic falsification that has enjoyed enormous popularity among sentimentalists of every era.

But while the poverty of little cottages may be disguised by the painters and writers who romanticize it, real poverty is not so easily charmed away. Nor, the poem implies, is real death. For the forty who 'come back no more' there has been no 'miracle.' To avoid the children's innocently-posed question is to act like children ourselves. That is, it is to deny the reality before our eyes in favour of the make-believe our elders tell us.

At the heart of 'Glee—The great storm is over,' as at the heart of Dickinson's entire confrontation with religion, lies the question raised by death. In its simplest form it is an age-old question: if God is both all-powerful and all-good, why are there evils such as death in the world? Why, if God's arm is long enough, does He not save? The most obvious answers to this question are either God's arm is not long enough (an answer Dickinson almost never gives) or that He is not willing. It is this latter possibility—a possibility evaded by sentimentalists but much dwelt upon by Puritans—that haunts and torments the poet's imagination. She returns to it again and again, using it to play havoc with both sentimentalist and, as we shall see, Puritan assumptions.

In 'Glee—The great storm is over,' Dickinson challenges sentimentalized faith on two levels: first on the level of language and, then, more deeply, on the level of teleology. Linguistically-speaking the poem's irony is blatant. Why 'Glee'? Why 'Salvation'? What do we have to 'Ring' (joyfully) about when there are so many 'bonnie' (from *bon*, good) souls for whom the bell 'toll[s]' (counts up as well as rings)?

As it is told (tolled), the miraculous story is a lie, a fiction, designed, like other sentimental fictions, to keep us from seeing and speaking the truth: it 'softens' and 'silences' our eyes and tongues. In doing so, it epitomizes the layers of rationalization by means of which sentimental believers are able to escape the difficulties inherent in their faith. To Dickinson, these difficulties point to the abyss, the engulfing/silencing sea, which represents not only our ignorance of God's true nature, intentions and purposes, but the possibility that there is no purpose at all. From this perspective, the very fabric of the sentimentalists' faith is fictitious, for it is composed of words—and events—that have been twisted from their 'true' meaning. And the sentimentalists' responses (grief, rage, joy) have been twisted with them. No *felix culpa* here.

Like her Puritan forebears—and distinctly unlike many of her own contemporaries—Dickinson was, in short, prepared to look God's 'evil' squarely in the face. The death of the young and the innocent, of neighbor and bridegroom, was no 'kindly' act to her. Nor were life's bitter 'lessons' something over which one had cause to rejoice, illustrations, as it were, of God's loving providence. In a second, somewhat later poem, also published early (1896), Dickinson makes a brutal pastiche out of the way sentimentalists think. Written like 'Glee—The great storm is over,' so that it can be read in two ways, the Blakean 'Far from Love the/Heavenly Father' is a bitter send-up of a standard nineteenth-century mother's prayer. I've taken such a prayer at random from May's anthology:

Far from Love the
Heaveny Father
Leads the Chosen
Child,
Oftener though Realm
of Briar
Than the Meadow
mild
Oftener by the Claw of
Dragon
Than the Hand of Friend
Guides the Little One
predestined
To the Native L   —
        (#1021, F,1242)

Still thy Guardian and thy Guide
Will be ever at thy side;
He will bring thee on thy way,
Through the cares of every day,
Till, when this life's trials o'er,
Thou standest on death's awful shore,
These dreams that nightly come to thee,
Prove thine in blest reality.

        (May 522)

Both these poems assume a deity whose primary concern is to guide and guard the 'Chosen Child' in his/her journey toward heaven, but in every other respect they could not be more unlike. To the author of the second poem, God is a totally domesticated figure, obviously identified with the mother herself in the loving care He is expected to exercise throughout the child's life. To Dickinson, He is a 'Dragon' (from *dracon*, snake) leading the child through realms of briar. Since Satan is specifically identified with the Dragon in Revelations, one of Dickinson's favorite biblical books, her poem's inverted message seems clear. 'God!—what a great and awful word!' Jane Taylor exclaims in a poem place-marked in *Hymns for Mothers and Children*, an anthology of sentimental verses owned by the Dickinson family, 'And yet a little child may bend,/And say, "my Father and my Friend".'[16] To Taylor, this 'awful' deity was a child's trusted 'Father and . . . Friend,' not to Dickinson.

'Far from Love' appears to be (and may well have been) Dickinson's angry response to such platitudes. By juxtaposing the Puritan conception of deity and life's trials with their sentimentalist revision, the poet has illuminated the folly and inadequacy of the latter approach. Given the facts of life, God is not our loving father nor does he act kindly toward us. On the contrary, most frequently he appears in the guise of our enemy, doing us wrong. '[W]hat "would be infinitely wicked for the highest angel in heaven",' Ann Douglas writes, quoting the Puritan theologian Joseph Bellamy, 'much less man . . . is "infinitely becoming to God". God . . . is absolutely entitled to commit what humanity calls crimes and account them benevolence; mankind must abide by his values.'[17] Put another way, mankind must endure God's perverse notion of what it means to be our 'Friend.'

Yet if this poem indicates that Dickinson had little sympathy with the sentimentalists' notion of God-our-loving-Father, 'Far from Love' also suggests she had just as little sympathy with the Puritans' conception of a Draconian sovereign God. The 'conflict between masculine Calvinism and feminized sentimentalism,'[18] which, as Levi St. Armand observes, characterizes Dickinson's era, was in many ways a struggle between ethical points of view. If the Puritan/Calvinist conception of God matched the 'evil' in the world better than his 'feminized' successor, the fact remained that this was only because the Puritans had accepted evil as part of God's plan. As the passages from Foster and Channing quoted earlier suggest, this was the vulnerability of the Puritans' theodicy, and it was one that Dickinson, like the sentimentalists, was clearly writing in reaction to.

In her recent biography of the poet, Cynthia Griffin Wolff has argued that Dickinson had both personal and generic reasons for engaging in what amounted to a lifelong wrestling match with 'God.'[19] On the one hand, as a woman and, equally important, as Austin's sister, Dickinson, Wolff claims, felt herself to have been unfairly treated by God. And like her biblical hero, Jacob, she was determined to use her 'cunning' (that is, her 'magic art' as well as 'knowledge,' with possibly a side glance at *cunnus*, vulva) to win the blessing her older brother (Austin/the male poet/men) had by birthright. In 'A little East of Jordan' (#59, F,111), which Wolff takes as Dickinson's signature poem, the poet fuses the story of Jacob and Esau with the separate and independent story of Jacob and the angel to make her situation clear. Like Esau, the angel in her poem cares more for his 'Breakfast' (pottage) than he does for winning. As a result, 'cunning' Jacob is able to compel him to give the blessing (the birthright) God has denied. For Dickinson it was the too-much-loved older brother's desire for 'pottage'—his worldly values—that gave the poet-pugilist her advantage over him. Austin might walk off with the family fortune (her father's name and law practice), but, as Wolff insists, Dickinson had her eye on higher things.[20]

But in identifying with Jacob, Dickinson had more general concerns as well. For it was not only she as woman who had been wronged by God (the idea behind poems such as 'Over the fence' [#251] and 'So I pull my Stockings off' [#1201]). *Vis-à-vis* this transcendent masculine deity, all humanity was female and in need of defense. Read 'correctly' (that is, through Dickinson's

Jacobean lens), the Bible tells the story of God's injustice, not his justice, of his cruelty, not his loving care. It is this lens, a lens molded by her Puritan precursors, but one they would have hanged her as a witch for using as she does—that Dickinson employs in poem after poem, as she takes God to task for the arbitrariness of His ways:

It always felt to me—a
wrong
To that Old Moses—done—
To let him see—the Canaan—
Without the entering—

And tho' in soberer moments—
No Moses there can be
I'm satisfied—the Romance
In point of injury—

Surpasses sharper stated—
Of Stephen—or of Paul—
For these—were only put to
death—
While God's adroiter will

On Moses—seemed to fasten
+With tantalizing Play + in
As Boy—should deal with
lesser Boy—
To +prove ability.

The fault—was doubtless
Israel's—
Myself—had banned the Tribes—
And ushered Grand Old
Moses
In Pentateuchal Robes

Upon the Broad Possession
+'Twas little—He should see—
Old Man on Nebo! Late as
this—
+My justice bleeds—for Thee!

+show supremacy   +Lawful Manor—
+But titled Him—to see—   +One—
(#597, F,551–2)

In a poem such as this, Dickinson is explicitly pitting
herself against *both* sentimental *and* Puritan conceptions
of God. To the sentimentalist, Moses' story was one of
loving self-sacrifice and the patriarch's reward lay in
heaven. 'For them, for them, but not for me,' Moses de-
clares in Jessie G. M'Cartee's poem, 'The Death of
Moses.' ' "[T]is well, my task is done,/Since Israel's sons
are blest;/Father, receive thy dying one/To thy eternal
rest!"' (May 156).

In M'Cartee's poem, the aw(e)fulness of God's deci-
sion to exclude Moses from Canaan, an aw(e)fulness in
which the Puritan fathers may be said to have gloried, is
utterly lost, as is any recognition of the divine unfairness
implicit in the exclusion itself. Indeed, in the entire
twelve stanzas, M'Cartee gives no indication that she
knows a problem exists. Moses' death occurs, as it were,
in a vacuum, a gratuitous—obviously feminized—self-
sacrifice that does not have to be explained since
it conforms so well to the social expectations put
upon women and their self-sacrificing male spiritual
leaders.

Yet if Dickinson reverts to an older understanding of
the implications of the exclusion, she hardly exhibits the
appropriately self-humiliating stance sinners were sup-
posed to assume when confronted with the judgment of
an angry God. On the contrary, her contempt for deity

could not be more plain. Pointing the reader to higher biblical criticism, she assumes its veracity without feeling any need to justify her position, and flips Moses' death on end, making it speak a very different truth: God is not a loving father. Nor is He sublimely Other. He is a bully and we are His victims. That is the true message of the 'Old Man's' story. It is one that we—as God's victims—have every right to protest against.[21]

To Dickinson, the existence of evils such as exclusion from Canaan, arbitrary disinheritance, pain, loss and death could not be made acceptable by self-humiliating definitions of divine sovereignty ('supremacy') any more than they could be relieved by the hope of salvation in some future life. Rather, the only rationally-consistent way to understand these evils was as the direct result of God's delight in human suffering and His need to prove His power. Taken as we experience His 'pleasure,' God is a sadist who thrives on the blood of human misery. It is we who martyr ourselves for Him—not He for us—pulling our tribute (in both senses of the term) dripping from our breast.

Sang from the Heart,
Sire,
Dipped My Beak in
it,
If the Tune drip too
much
Have a tint too Red

Pardon the Cochineal—
Suffer the Vermillion—
Death is the Wealth
Of the Poorest Bird.

Bear with the Ballad—
Awkward—faltering—
Death twists the strings—
'Twasn't my blame—

Pause in your Liturgies—
Wait your Chorals—
While I +repeat your
Hallowed name—

+recite

(#1059, F,1122–3)

In the continual chant of praise which in Book III of
Paradise Lost composes Milton's version of the harmony
of heaven—God's song of praise for himself sung by his
obedient, self-mirroring disciples—there is no room for
the small sad voice of human suffering.[22] Indeed, Dickin-
son claims, should that suffering call attention to itself
(be too 'Vermillion,' too 'loud' a color), it will only earn
disapproval, not compassion, from our 'Sire' (both
Sovereign and Father) in the sky.

In one of her most moving and powerful poems,
'Behind me dips Eternity,' Dickinson makes the gulf
between the existential reality of (female) human suffer-
ing and the impervious narcissism of divine (masculine)
perfection, suggested in 'Sang from the Heart,/Sire,' the
specific focus of her text. We are the term 'between,' the
beings who—to paraphrase God's curse on Adam and
Eve—bear our children in sorrow and eat the bread of
sorrow all our days. Whatever 'miracles' lie 'behind' and
'before' us—whether eternity or immortality—these
states do nothing to alleviate the darkness enveloping
our lives. Like the 'Crescent in the Sea' (the female
moon), we wax and wane. Above us, around us, the
storm rages.

Behind Me—dips Eternity—
Before Me—Immortality—
Myself—the Term between—
Death but the Drift of
Eastern Gray,
Dissolving into Dawn away,
before the West begin—

'Tis Kingdoms—afterward—they
say—
In perfect—pauseless Monarchy—
Whose Prince—is Son of None—
Himself—His Dateless Dynasty—
Himself—Himself diversify—
In Duplicate divine—

'Tis Miracle before Me—then—
'Tis Miracle behind—between—
A Crescent in the Sea—
With Midnight to the
North of Her—
And Midnight to the
South of Her—
And Maelstrom—in the Sky—

(#721, F,879–80)

It is unlikely that the cold chill evoked by the second
stanza of this poem with its self-mirroring repetitions
and alliterations and cool abstract language (so utterly
unlike the supposed warmth of the sentimentalists'
domesticated heaven) can be matched anywhere in
Dickinson's canon. The kingdom of Christ, that 'Son of
None,' is not a place of human peace and satisfaction. It
is merely the 'pauseless' mirror in which God, through a
process of infinite regression, duplicates 'Himself.' Like
a circle (or a zero or a snake eating its own tail), God's
'Dateless Dynasty' is self-enclosed and totally self-

absorbed. When we die, we too will be absorbed into it, forgetting the suffering that defines our lives and makes us, by that same token, what we are. 'She was scarcely the aunt you knew,' Dickinson wrote to the Norcross cousins shortly after her mother's death in 1882,

> The great mission of pain had been ratified—cultivated to tenderness by persistent sorrow, so that a larger mother died than had she died before. There was no earthly parting. She slipped from our fingers like a flake gathered by the wind, and is now part of the drift called "the infinite."
> We don't know where she is, though so many tell us.
>
> (L,750)

Dickinson goes on to tell her cousins that she is sure we will be 'cherished by our Maker' after our death, but God's is, clearly, a cold embrace. It is suffering that has made the mother larger and at the same time more fully human. Once absorbed into the chill drifts of eternity, this poor solitary human flake will lose not only her location but her identity and name. '[W]e are to have no Face [body?] in a farther Life,' Dickinson wrote to Charles H. Clark in 1883 (L,792), mourning the fact. To Mrs Henry Hills in 1884, she declared, 'When Jesus tells us about his Father, we distrust him. When he shows us his Home, we turn away, but when he confides to us that he is "acquainted with Grief," we listen, for that also is an Acquaintance of our own' (L,837).

As such statements indicate, Dickinson's awareness that suffering 'enlarges' us (makes us, not a little ironically, more human), did nothing to reconcile her to it. God gave us pain. He kept perfection to Himself. That was all. Unlike her sentimental poetess-peers she could not erase this pain in gratitude for life-everlasting—nor, like the Puritans, could she accept it as deserved punishment for sin. It was unfair. It was part of the general unfairness that God—the archetypal male bully—had structured into the universe. And it was this unfairness that Emily Dickinson's poems call into account.

Of the various inequities for which God was responsible none seems to have outraged Dickinson more than death. If Dickinson appears obsessed with death, it must be remembered that large numbers of middle-class women in her period were similarly, if not more, obsessed. 'To say that the memoirs of women and clergymen were concerned with death,' Ann Douglas writes, 'is an understatement; to a degree that requires special consideration, they were exercises in necrophilia.'[23] Given the conditions under which nineteenth-century women lived, however, their concern with death is not surprising.

As Cynthia Griffin Wolff observes, during the nineteenth century the medical profession could still do little to protect people from even the most common illnesses. An influenza or cold could turn deadly. And '[w]henever there was sickness in the house,' Wolff writes, 'the womenfolk (even if they were very young) were expected to be in attendance.'[24] Next to rearing children, tending the ill and dying was a middle-class woman's most important social function. She cared for the sick and laid out and mourned the dead—the largest number of whom came from among the children she bore. Given infant mortality rates and the rise in the incidence of childbed fever, it is no wonder, then, that nineteenth-century women's memoirs were fixated on mortuary subjects. Even apart from the inundation of casualties brought on by the Civil War, death was all around them, shaping and informing their daily lives.[25]

But if Dickinson was not unique in her obsession with death, she was unique in the degree to which she was prepared to protest, and protest vociferously, against it. Unlike her peers, she could not erase the reality of death in the expectation of life everlasting, nor could she alleviate its pain by contemplating heavenly rewards. Although she frequently depicts death as a figure of awe and power, a conferrer of 'degree,' her most settled attitude toward it is one of intense, almost violent, psychological rebellion at the loss it entails. Even in the early, highly sentimental 'Going to Heaven,' Dickinson is unwilling to let the world go. 'I'd like to look a little more/At such a curious Earth!' (#79, F,108), she coyly confides. By the time she reached maturity, her outrage knew no bounds and could not be more straightforwardly expressed:

The Frost of Death was on the Pane—
"Secure your Flower" said he.
Like Sailors fighting with a Leak
We fought Mortality.

Our passive Flower we held to Sea—
To Mountain—To the Sun—
Yet even on his Scarlet shelf
To crawl the Frost begun—

We pried him back
Ourselves we wedged
Himself and her between,
Yet easy as the narrow Snake
He forked his way along

Till all her helpless beauty bent
And then our wrath begun—
We hunted him to his Ravine
We chased him to his Den—

73

We hated Death and hated Life
And nowhere was to go—
Than Sea and continent there is
A larger—it is Woe

(#1136, P,797)

As (more subtly) in 'Because I could not stop for Death'
(#712) and 'A Visitor in Marl' (#391), death in this poem is
a form of rape. That is, it is an *intrusion into nature*, not an
aspect of it. Female in its beauty, but also in its powerless-
ness to protect itself against intrusion, the flower is cast in
the role of a romantic maiden in distress. Like a satanic
trinity, the snake is death, frost, and (presumably), the
devil in one. As such, it epitomizes the destructive poten-
tial which Dickinson seems to have believed was latent in
all forms of masculine power, including God's. It is God,
after all, who ordains death, frost, and snake—as well as
flowers. They are the instruments of His will, the means
through which His ordination comes to pass.

Like a knight in a medieval tale, or like a sailor fighting a
leak, the poet-pugilist attempts to rescue the 'helpless
beauty,' but neither her courage nor her wrath avail. Woe
is inevitable. 'Mortality'—in the secondary sense of the
term—cannot do without it. We are our loss. Our loss is
part of God's 'Perturbless Plan.' We do not even have the
right to speak out against it. If we do, God will not listen:

It's easy to invent a Life—
God does it—every Day—
Creation—but the Gambol
Of His Authority—

It's easy to efface it—
The thrifty Deity
Could scarce afford Eternity
To Spontaneity—

The Perished Patterns murmur—
But His Perturbless Plan
Proceed—inserting Here—
a Sun—
There—leaving out a Man—

(#724, F,883)

The man dies. The sun (and Son) shines. The unmoved
mover moves on. Whatever was taken—be it flower or
bird, soldier or loved one—all Dickinson could see was
the waste, a waste without which earth itself would have
sufficed, the only paradise human beings needed:

His Bill is clasped—his Eye forsook—
His Feathers wilted low—
The Claws that clung, like lifeless Gloves
Indifferent hanging now—
The Joy that in his happy Throat
Was waiting to be poured
Gored through and through with Death, to be
Assassin of a Bird
Resembles to my outraged mind
The firing in Heaven
On Angels—squandering for you
Their Miracles of Tune

1. clasped] locked   6. Was waiting] Assembled
1. forsook] estranged   12. Miracles of] unsuspecting/[unsus-]
4. hanging] gathered   picious

(#1102, P, 775)

In *Paradise Lost*, the fallen angels employ gunpowder,
firing on the heavenly host. In heaven the damage is
repairable. On earth it is not. Like the 'Perished Patterns'
of 'It's easy to invent a Life,' the bird is dead, its 'Miracles
of Tune' permanently squandered by a God who willed
it so, a God who gambles as well as gambols with his
creation. 'Except for it's marauding Hand,' Dickinson

75

noted to Higginson on the death of his brother, 'it had been Heaven below—' (L,494). This theme reverberates through all her writing—the basic unfairness and ultimate cruelty of a God who gave all only to take it away, a God whose 'Perturbless Plan' makes Him seem more serpent (or Dragon) than 'Friend' to those who worship Him. Callous and (as Wolff notes) more than a little satanic in His role as 'inventor,'[26] this God is deaf to the music His creation makes.

Dickinson's rage against death, a rage that led her at times to hate both life and death, might have been alleviated, had she been able to gather hard evidence about an afterlife. But, of course, she could not. 'The *Bareheaded life*—under the grass—,' she wrote to Samuel Bowles in *c.* 1860, 'worries one like a Wasp' (L,364). If death was the gate to a better life in 'the childhood of the kingdom of Heaven,' as the sentimentalists—and Christ—claimed, then, perhaps, there was compensation and healing for life's woes. In a poem such as 'I shall know why—when Time is over' (#193), Dickinson explores this possibility, deliberately adopting the 'naïve' childlike voice that faith in God's ultimate goodness and explicability requires, and ironically undercutting that faith as a result. But how do we know? What can we know? In 'I heard a Fly buzz—when/I died,' Dickinson concludes that we do not know much:

I heard a Fly buzz—when
I died—
The Stillness in the Room
Was like the Stillness in the Air—
Between the Heaves of Storm—

The Eyes around—had wrung them
dry—
And Breaths were gathering firm
For that last Onset—when the King
Be witnessed—in the Room—

I willed my Keepsakes—Signed away
What portion of me be
Assignable—and then it was
There interposed a Fly—

With Blue—uncertain—stumbling Buzz—
Between the light—and me—
And then the Windows failed—and then
I could not see to see—

(#465, F,591)

Like many people in her period, Dickinson was fascinated by death-bed scenes. How, she asked various correspondents, did this or that person die? In particular, she wanted to know if their deaths revealed any information about the nature of the afterlife. In this poem, however, she imagines her own death-bed scene, and the answer she provides is grim, as grim (and, at the same time, as ironically mocking), as anything she ever wrote.

In the narrowing focus of death, the fly's insignificant buzz, magnified tenfold by the stillness in the room, is all that the speaker hears. This kind of distortion in scale is common. It is one of the 'illusions' of perception. But here it is horrifying because it defeats every expectation we have. Death is supposed to be an experience of awe. It is the moment when the soul, departing the body, is taken up by God. Hence the watchers at the bedside wait for the moment when the 'King' (whether God or death) 'be witnessed' in the room. And hence the speaker assigns away everything but that which she expects God (her soul) or death (her body) to take.

77

What arrives instead, however, is neither God nor death but a fly, '[w]ith Blue—uncertain—stumbling Buzz,' a fly, that is, no more secure, no more sure, than we are. Dickinson had associated flies with death once before in the exquisite lament, 'How many times these low feet/staggered.' In this poem, they buzz 'on the/ chamber window,' and speckle it with dirt (#187, F,152), reminding us that the housewife, who once protected us from such intrusions, will protect us no longer. Their presence is threatening but only in a minor way, 'dull' like themselves. They are a background noise we do not have to deal with yet.

In 'I heard a Fly buzz,' on the other hand, there is only one fly and its buzz is not only foregrounded. Before the poem is over, the buzz takes up the entire field of perception, coming between the speaker and the 'light' (of day, of life, of knowledge). It is then that the 'Windows' (the eyes that are the windows of the soul as well as, metonymically, the light that passes through the panes of glass) 'fail' and the speaker is left in darkness—in death, in ignorance. She cannot 'see' to 'see' (understand).

Given that the only sure thing we know about 'life after death' is that flies—in their adult form and more particularly, as maggots—devour us, the poem is at the very least a grim joke. In projecting her death-bed scene, Dickinson confronts her ignorance and gives back the only answer human knowledge can with any certainty give. While we may hope for an afterlife, no one, not even the dying, can prove it exists.

Like 'Four Trees—upon a solitary/Acre,' 'I heard a Fly buzz' represents an extreme position. I believe that to Dickinson it was a position that reduced human life to too elementary and meaningless a level. Abdicating belief, cutting off God's hand, as in 'I heard a Fly buzz' (a poem that tests precisely this situation), leaves us with nothing. Not just God, but we ourselves are reduced—a fact that has become painfully evident in twentieth-century literature, as Dickinson in one poem seems to predict:

Those—dying then,
Knew where they went—
They went to God's Right Hand—
That Hand is amputated now
And God cannot be found—

The abdication of Belief
Makes the Behavior small—
Better an ignis fatuus
Than no illume at all—

(#1551, P,1069)

Whether or not this poem was written as a response to Charles Wadsworth's death, as Johnson suggests,[27] it is a strikingly bitter piece. But it also points to a vital truth. By 1882, its presumed date of composition, the combined forces of Darwinism, higher biblical criticism and social revolution had undermined the foundations of religious faith, and sentimentalism, for all its efforts, was not able to patch it together. In a very real sense, God was dead.

But although she tested God severely, Dickinson could not let Him die. Owning, as she said, a faith 'That doubts as fervently as it believes' (#1144, P,803), like an electrical charge, she oscillates instead between the two poles of faith and doubt, making poetry from each. A year after she wrote 'Those—dying then' (c. 1882), she sent Maria Whitney 'To the bright east she flies,' one of her most exquisite elegies, on her mother:

To the bright east she flies,
Brothers of Paradise
Remit her home,
Without a change of wings,
Or Love's convenient things,
Enticed to come.

Fashioning what she is,
Fathoming what she was,
We deem we dream—
And that dissolves the days
Through which existence strays
Homeless at home.

(#1573, P,1084)

There is no bitterness in this poem, nor disbelief—only a poignant recognition of how distant and alienated we are from what could well be our true 'home,' and how alienated (estranged) from our life on earth we are because of it. The dead, Macbeth declares, are happy. 'After life's fitful fever' they sleep (III.ii.23). But we, who are alive, wander through existence, 'Homeless at home,' not quite belonging to one world or sure of the other, strangers to both. To Dickinson, it was precisely this situation (this divided consciousness, this awareness of two possible kinds of 'life') that made us human, investing our lives—and deaths—with a peculiar and inimitable tragedy no other creature shared:

Where every bird is bold to go
And bees abashless play,
The foreigner before he knocks
Must thrust the tears away.

(#1758, P,1179)

If there is a single unifying theme in Dickinson's religious poetry, it lies here—in the poet's recognition

that it is our ignorance and fear, not our eventual sal-
vation, our sorrow and pain, not our future bliss, that in
religious terms comprise the defining conditions of our
lives. Born in ignorance, we at once know too much and
not enough. And hence we will always be 'foreigners' in
whatever land we travel, divided by our awareness of
death from complete absorption into the world in which
we live, yearning for another life whose existence we can
never prove. Finally, death is the irrevocable song we
hear, the song whose hearing separates us from all other
beings in creation.

For Dickinson to abandon totally a belief in an afterlife
(a belief in God's saving hand) would have been tanta-
mount to giving up hope that we might have any 'home'
at all:

Further in Summer than the Birds
Pathetic from the Grass
A minor Nation celebrates
It's unobtrusive Mass.

No Ordinance be seen
So gradual the Grace
A pensive Custom it becomes
Enlarging Loneliness.

Antiquest felt at Noon
When August burning low
Arise this spectral Canticle
Repose to typify

Remit as yet no Grace
No Furrow on the Glow
Yet a Druidic Difference
Enhances Nature now

(#1068, P,752)

Her crickets, Dickinson told Thomas Niles, are 'a chill

Gift,' (L,768), their strange song a sacrament of death, 'Repose to typify.' But it is only the human listener, the focus of this poem, who understands the full implications of the mystery their singing celebrates and who longs for the security of another life as a result. And it is only the dead who know whether or not this afterlife exists:

> Pass to thy Rendezvous of Light,
> Pangless except for us—
> Who slowly ford the Mystery
> Which thou has leaped across!
> (#1564, P,1078)

'Hamlet,' Dickinson wrote in 1877, 'wavered for all of us' (L,587).

In *The Only Kangaroo Among the Beauty*, Karl Keller suggests that it was the very Puritanism of Dickinson's faith that moved her to wrestle so with God; but she did so with a difference.[28] Dickinson's questions do not relate to the status of her own soul. Whether or not she believed herself saved, rarely if ever after the letters of late adolescence does she express personal concern for sin or for her own salvation.[29] Nor, as I discuss in the next chapter, did she see nature as fallen and in need of grace.

It was the Creator—not the creation—whose actions required forgiveness and it was His injustices and inequities that she wrestled with all her life. By the end of her life, she, the pugilist, the woman ready to test her concept of God against the Bible's word, just as she tested her knowledge of how things were against the 'wisdom of the ages,' was ready to bless Him. It is a testimony to the depth of her faith and the ultimate triumph of her life—to the 'audacity of [her] Bliss'—that she could. Why she could, despite her deep-rooted scepticism regarding both the goodness of God's intentions and the reality of our knowledge of them, will be the subject I look at next.

Chapter Three

Vinnie's Garden

There is not yet Frost, and Vinnie's Garden
from the Door looks like a Pond, with Sunset on it.
Bathing in that heals her.
How simple is Bethesda!

(Dickinson to Mrs Holland, 1877)

When in need of healing, it was not to the consolations of religion that Emily Dickinson turned but to the consolations of nature. 'Expulsion from Eden grows indistinct in the presence of flowers so blissful, and with no disrespect to Genesis, Paradise remains,' (L,610) she wrote Mrs Thomas P. Field in 1878, acknowledging a gift of flowers. In the wider context of Dickinson's work, the comment was more than graceful hyperbole. Whatever credit attached to the story of our 'expulsion from Eden,' the natural world remained and the natural world was a place of wondrous beauty. Looking on this beauty (bathing in its bliss) healed the poet's spirit in precisely the same way that the ancient Hebrews healed their bodies by bathing in the pond at Bethesda (L,593). As a type for paradise, the earth would do.

In poems and notes sent to her nephews, especially to Ned, Dickinson delights in nothing more than presenting herself as the apostle of a new 'religion,' one that 'captivates' rather than condemns. Drawn from nature, not the Bible, this religion was free from all taint of Adam's transgression and from the consequent need for atonement. As a result, it won us to love God not through fear but wonder, for it emphasized the beauty and bliss of the Creator's creation, not the terrifying, or even the paradoxically fortunate, consequences of sin.

When writing to her nephews, Dickinson tended to characterize her point of view as a 'boy's' religion, apparently in the belief that it was only as boys 'faded' into men that they lost touch with their true feelings and became the ghostly mouthpieces for patriarchal law. As she observes in a poem sent to Ned after he skipped church one Sunday, it was men, not boys, who were responsible for the story of the fall.[1] And it was men who felt righteously entitled to divide humanity into the saved and damned as a result. Men have a vested interest in keeping traditional religion going. Boys—and, presumably, women—do not.

> The Bible is an antique Volume—
> Written by faded Men
> At the suggestion of Holy Spectres—
> Subjects—Bethlehem—
> Eden—the ancient Homestead—
> Satan—the Brigadier—
> Judas—the Great Defaulter—
> David—the Troubadour—
> Sin—a distinguished Precipice
> Others must resist—

Boys that "believe" are very lonesome—
Other Boys are "lost"—
Had but the Tale a warbling Teller—
All the Boys would come—
Orpheus's Sermon captivated—
It did not condemn—

(#1545, P,1065–6)

As Cynthia Griffin Wolff has argued, it was the church's invasiveness—its demand for total spiritual capitulation—that led Dickinson to reject it in the end.[2] 'How strange that Nature does not knock, and yet does not intrude' (L,587), the poet wrote to Mrs James S. Cooper in 1877, respecting a gift of flowers, given or received. In the same vein, after the death of Samuel Bowles in 1878, Dickinson sent flowers to his mistress, Maria Whitney, with a note declaring, 'Intrusiveness of flowers is brooked by even troubled hearts./They enter and then knock. . . ./May these molest as fondly!' (L,603).

If nature's consolations molested 'fondly,' Dickinson did not feel the same way about the consolations offered by the church. On the contrary, with its stories of sin, damnation and repentance and its deliberate encouragement of overwrought emotional states, what the church did appears—in her mind—to have been closer to rape. After a brief period of adolescent confusion, following her attendance at revival meetings, the poet never exposed herself so openly again. Playing wittily on the iconographic tradition that depicts the Holy Ghost as a dove, she claims that it is from the 'warbling' throat of a bird that we best learn of God, not from faded men. In nature, we discover another and preferable source of divine 'revelation,' a more loving and lovable (because less intrusive, less battering) 'God.'

In the semi-final draft of 'The Bible is an antique Volume'—here titled 'Diagnosis of the Bible, by a Boy'—Dickinson provides thirteen variants for the 'warbling' she finally selected: thrilling, typic, hearty, bonnie, breathless, spacious, tropic, ardent, friendly, magic, pungent, winning and mellow. God's 'song' as we know it in nature, from the bubbling throat of the Bobolink, is all these things and more; but we must shut our ears to the church and to the biblical stories in order to hear it. Alienated from traditional religion as much by the intrusiveness of its masculinism as by the intrusiveness of its message, Dickinson was prepared to shut her ears in this way.

Dickinson's move to a nature-based religion was an extraordinarily canny solution to the dilemma confronting her. As we have seen, nineteenth-century sentimentalism sought to soften the (masculine) aggressiveness of the Calvinist/Puritan deity by domesticating God. In clinging to the outward trappings of orthodoxy, however, sentimentalism had tied itself to the past. No matter how rationalized, its image of God could not be freed from the contradictions contained within the biblical stories (any more than it could be separated from the real evil in the world). As a result, sentimentalized religion was subverted by the very source meant to legitimate its truth. God might be our 'kindly Father,' but, as Dickinson was at pains to point out, He was still more 'Dragon' than 'Friend' to those who loved Him.

As a base from which to draw God's image, nature, on the other hand, was free from the biblical baggage. More than that, nature was also (traditionally) a woman or, as Dickinson calls her in a number of poems, a 'mother' (#s 790, 1085, 1115 and 1143). She could therefore *legitimately* bring to the image of God the very qualities of nurturance and loving care sentimentalism could introduce only by covert, self-subverting means. Nature offered, consequently, a free-standing alternative to the traditional (masculinist) concept of God. *In potentia*, it also offered a way around the entire masculinist tradition. By defining God in terms of nature, Dickinson was able to assert a fully separate and autonomous source for female power—something sentimental writers, for all their domesticity, could never do. Immanent in nature, this image of God became Dickinson's answer to the killing transcendence of the biblical deity and, at the same time, a basis on which to claim a (female) power of her own.

For Dickinson's poetry, this latter consequence was crucial. Like nature itself, women within the masculinist tradition (whether religious or poetic) were denied a voice. Marginalized by their subordinate status, they were muted by it as well. In Dickinson's 'Diagnosis' of the Bible (there is indeed a 'disease' there), women do not appear. In the sentimentalist revision of orthodoxy, female values are still subordinate to and subsumed by male power. Women have a voice, but only to reinforce the cultural stereotypes that limit and marginalize them in various ways. Thus, for example, in that tome of popular sentiment, *The Mother's Journal and Family Visitant*, PHB writes of Mary, that she is 'the same *unassuming woman* in every situation—strictly adhering to the path of duty, whatever sacrifice of feeling it might cost her.'[3] She may be the mother of God, but unassumingness (silence, acceptance of marginalization) remained the signature of the true Christian woman.

Viewed in respect to nature alone, however—that is, outside the Bible and the masculinist tradition—female qualities could become autonomous sources of power and truth. 'Your intimacy with the Mountains I heartily endorse—,' Dickinson wrote Ned, less than a year before her death. 'Ties more Eleusinian I must leave to you—

Deity will guide you—I do not mean Jehovah—The little God with the Epaulettes I spell it in French to conceal it's temerity' (L,880). Despite her final caveat, Dickinson was hardly concealing her 'temerity.' The Eleusinian mysteries were the mysteries of Demeter and Persephone. To participate in these (mother) rites, she tells her young disciple, he need only take nature (the unnamed alternative deity) as his guide.

In what Sandra Gilbert appropriately calls a 'matriarchal prayer,'[4] Dickinson, the 'wayward nun' of Puritan New England, carries the woman- or mother-centeredness of her nature-based religion as far as it will go. Making a submerged identification between the blunt rounded shape of the western Massachusetts mountains and a woman's breasts, Dickinson presents nature, embodied in these mountains, as the 'strong Madonna,' from whom she sucks support. Like a baby in her mother's arms, the poet looks up across the maternal hills to meet her mother's 'far—slow—Violet Gaze—.' The mother-child dyad controlling the poem (an ironic play on conventional nineteenth-century portraits of the Madonna and Child), is perfectly posed and in itself complete, a 'service' requiring no other, least of all the 'little God with the Epaulettes.'[5]

Sweet Mountains—Ye tell Me
no lie—
Never deny Me—Never fly—
Those same unvarying Eyes
Turn on Me—when I fail—
or feign,
Or take the Royal names
in vain—
Their far—slow—Violet Gaze—

My Strong Madonnas—
Cherish still—
The Wayward Nun—beneath
the Hill—
Whose service—is to You—
Her latest Worship—When
the Day
Fades from the Firmament
away—
To lift Her Brows on You—
                    (#722, F,881)

Dickinson is not subverting an androcentric concept of God in this poem. She is jettisoning it altogether and reconstructing God in woman's image. 'God' *is* the mother in whose unvarying gaze we may put our trust. She will not deny us, no more than our earthly mothers would, even if we fail. She is as beautiful and everlasting as the mountains to whom the speaker prays. If Dickinson called herself a 'Pagan' as she grew older, such poems may explain why.

This poem also makes clear, however, that for Dickinson, God *could be* loving and lovable, but only in a female or immanent form. And it was in this form—in nature— that the poet loved 'Him.' For here 'He' ceased to threaten and became beautiful and winning: 'mellow,' 'pungent,' 'tropic,' 'friendly,' and 'ardent,' instead. With all its variety and intensity—its extraordinary fusion of close observation with intuitive, even mystical response— Dickinson's nature poetry is a testament to this love. Given its emphasis on female and, in particular, on 'domestic' values, it is also a testament to the ultimately positive effect that woman-centered sentimentalism had upon her. This chapter will examine the way in which Dickinson used the conventions of sentimental nature poetry, especially as they were employed by women, to create poems that were distinctly hers yet at the same time the products of a female artistic tradition. It will then look at how Dickinson filled these conventions with the inebriating 'wine' of her own nature 'religion,' her private 'communion in the Haze' (#130, F,101).

As Wendy Martin observes, like other bourgeois women of her period, Dickinson engaged in the sentimental sharing of nature throughout her life.[6] In keeping with the Victorian customs of their times, middle-class women exchanged gifts of fruits and flowers, notes on natural phenomena, bits of natural artifacts (leaves, feathers, twigs and the like) and art work depicting natural forms or made of natural materials—some, such as crosses of flowers, quite astonishingly elaborate.[7]

In *Aurora Leigh*, Elizabeth Barrett Browning satirizes the excesses involved in such activities, especially as they affected the education of young girls in England:

I danced the polka and Cellarius,
Spun glass, stuffed birds, and modelled flowers in wax,
Because she liked accomplishments in girls,[8]

But trivial as these 'accomplishments' may seem to Barrett Browning (or, for that matter, to us), they suggest that women's relationship to nature in this period was functionally quite different from that of men. Broadly-speaking, whatever the area of their interest—whether religion, science, philosophy, or art—men went to nature to discover the principles or spirit behind it. 'Nature,' Louis Agassiz writes in 'Methods of Study in Natural History,' serialized in the 1862 *Atlantic Monthly*, 'is the work of thought, the production of intelligence carried out according to plan, therefore premeditated,—and in our study of natural objects we are approaching the thoughts of the Creator, reading His conceptions, interpreting a system that is His and not ours.'[9] To grasp this rational order (whether as a set of scientific laws or as the apprehension of the ideal) required, as Emerson put it, 'manly contemplation of the whole.'[10]

While it is unlikely that many nineteenth-century women would have disagreed with Agassiz's statement on the relationship between God and nature, their *experience* of nature was very different from his—or from that of men generally in this period. Largely empirical and confined to daily life, it was smaller in scale, more immersed in detail and more domestically-oriented than the experience of men. It came to them through their routine activities, cooking and gardening, as much as through their desire to acquire 'accomplishments.' And as a result, women tended to see nature, especially material nature, in a more intimate and confiding way, the more so since, like men, they gendered nature as female.

Indeed, what is most striking about American women's statements on nature in this period is the degree to which these writers were prepared both to trust nature and to identify with her. In *Nature*, Emerson, for example, takes what may fairly be called the 'classical' male position on nature, exhibiting the traditional anxieties which have shaped the Platonic heritage toward physical nature in the West:

But this beauty of Nature which is seen and felt as beauty, is the least part. The shows of day, the dewy morning, the rainbow, mountains, orchards in blossom, stars, moonlight, shadows in still water, and the like, if too eagerly hunted, become shows merely, and mock us with their unreality. Go out of the house to see the moon, and 't is mere tinsel; it will not please. . . . The beauty that shimmers in the yellow afternoons of October, who ever could clutch it? Go forth to find it, and it is gone; 't is only a mirage. . . .

To love such beauty, Emerson warns, is a form of 'effeminacy.' It is only '[t]he high and divine beauty,'[11] the unchanging ideal, that, he argues, is the proper subject of the masculine mind. Keenly aware of his own masculine identity, like other men writing within this tradition from Plato on, Emerson's approach to nature is, as Margaret Homans observes, distrustful and appropriative at once.[12] To Emerson, physical nature (conceived of in female terms, even when not so labelled) is something outside the self, to be studied, controlled and, finally, transcended, that her 'tinsel' might not prove too alluring.

For the anonymous female author of *Leaf and Flower Pictures, and How to Make Them* (1857), on the other hand, nature and self cannot be separated. ' "Nature never did betray the heart that loved her," ' she quotes, 'and you will follow my directions, and catch my enthusiasm for these delightful pursuits, I am quite sure you will never feel disposed to sue me for a *"breach of promise."* '[13] As the confusion of subject and object in the latter part of this sentence suggests, for this author, as for women generally in this period, self and nature were one. Admonitions such as Emerson's notwithstanding, both could be trusted. If this writer's position is philosophically naïve (which it certainly is), it nevertheless gave her a basis on which to feel solidly at home in the ephemeral (material) world.

It was, perhaps, because nineteenth-century women did identify so closely with physical nature and experienced it in such an intimate and material way that women poets in this period write on topics drawn from nature with an unusual degree of freedom and success. As early as the 1830s, Sarah Josepha Hale, who would later bemoan the circumscription of themes and images in women's poetry, was still able to include 'sentiments' by a healthy number of women poets in *Flora's Interpreter: Or, The American Book of Flowers and Sentiments*. A direct product of the tradition which led women to put together calendars and dictionaries of flowers, Hale's text concludes with a small anthology of flower poems, half of which were written by women, Sigourney among them.[14]

As the century progressed, women not only contributed heavily to the literature of flowers and sentiments, but, in the pictorial mode of their time, produced books of poems and pictures, too—texts like Henrietta Dumont's, *The Floral Offering: A Token of Affection and Esteem; Comprising the Language and Poetry of Flowers*, 1851, Mrs C. M. Badger's *Wild Flowers Drawn and Colored from Nature*, presented to Dickinson by her father in 1859, and L. Clarkson's *Indian Summer: Autumn Poems and Sketches*, 1883, dedicated to Clarkson's mother in the 'Autumn' of her life.[15] Arising out of the very educational tradition Barrett Browning satirized, a tradition which demanded that young ladies 'sketch from nature well and study flowers,'[16] such texts testify eloquently to women's visual acuity and to their love of and familiarity with individual natural phenomena. Like nineteenth-century male poets in the United States, whose landscape 'painting' was also based on models provided by the visual arts (in particular, the Hudson River School), these women took their cue from the visual. But as Sigourney's 'Alpine Flowers,' in *Flora's Interpreter*, suggests, the model they used, the lady's sketchbook, led them to a very different emphasis and therefore to a different kind of art:

Meek dwellers mid yon terror-stricken cliffs!
With brows so pure, and incense-breathing lips,
Whence are ye? Did some white-winged messenger,
On Mercy's missions, trust your timid germ
To the cold cradle of eternal snows,
Or, breathing on the callous icicles,
Bid them with tear-drops nurse ye?
         Tree nor shrub
Dare that drear atmosphere; nor polar pine
Uprears a veteran front; yet there ye stand,
Leaning your cheeks against the thick-ribbed ice,
And looking up with brilliant eyes to Him
Who bids you bloom unblanched, amid the waste
Of desolation. Man, who, panting, toils
O'er slippery steeps, or, trembling, treads the verge
Of yawning gulfs, o'er which the headlong plunge
Into eternity, looks shuddering up,
And marks ye in your placid loveliness—
Fearless, yet frail—and, clasping his chill hands,
Blesses your pencilled beauty. Mid the pomp
Of mountain summits rushing to the sky,
And chaining the rapt soul in breathless awe,
He bows to bind you drooping to his breast,
Inhales your spirit from the frost-winged gale,
And freer dreams of heaven.[17]

Sigourney's poem is relatively unusual in women's nature poetry in its depiction of mountains; but the mountains are here only to offset her flowers. In this towering and aggressively masculine landscape—the kind of landscape in which male poets and artists sought the 'breathless awe' of the sublime—Sigourney chooses to focus on a single lowly detail (what Naomi Schor would call a female detail): the small white alpine flowers. For in their 'placid loveliness' and 'fearless' frailty, their purity and paradoxically stubborn strength, she has discovered not just a type heaven but also a type for her own woman self. Finally, she observes, it is to this meek, pure flower that 'panting' man in his search for salvation must bow, binding it 'to his breast.' If male poets and artists found the world, as Barton Levi St. Armand puts it, quoting Gerard Manley Hopkins, 'charged with the *grandeur* of God' (my italics),[18] Sigourney and other women poets learned to look to nature's small and seemingly insignificant moments (the kind they were most likely to sketch) for their intimations of immortality. As Hale said, speaking of the difference between her anthology and Cheever's *American Common-place Book of Poetry*, women offered up the 'roses,' while men devoted themselves to the 'evergreens,' of life ('grave and pious' thoughts).

It is within this female poetic and artistic tradition, a tradition that emphasized intimacy and detail, and valued the material and the ephemeral, that Emily Dickinson wrote. Like leaves torn from a lady's drawing pad, Dickinson's poems on natural subjects, ranging from bats and rats to summer days and snow storms, are brief epitomes drawn from the world in which she lived. They are 'sketches' of the beauties—or, sometimes, the grotesqueries—that surrounded her, Nature's 'meanest Tunes,' which she shared with her friends. Indeed, some of her nature poems read almost as if she had set herself exercises in writing them. This, for example, on a rainstorm, and, in particular, on the curious freshness and evanescence of the post-storm, ozone-laden air:

> It sounded as if the Streets were running
> And then—the Streets stood still—
> Eclipse—was all we could see at the Window
> And Awe—was all we could feel.

Vinnie's Garden

By and by—the boldest stole out of his Covert
To see if Time was there—
Nature was in an Opal Apron,
Mixing fresher Air.

(#1397, P,967)

'It sounded as if the Streets were running' is one of
twelve poems written between 1860 and 1883 (that is,
basically, from the beginning to the end of Dickinson's
writing career) in which the poet treats one or another
aspect of a rainstorm. In her earliest attempts—'On this
long storm the Rainbow rose' and 'An Awful Tempest
mashed the air'—her comparisons are forced. Clouds are
'listless Elephants' (#194, F,164); creatures gnash their
teeth and swing their 'frenzied/hair' (#198, F,170). By
1877, the presumed date of 'It sounded as if the Streets
were running,' she knew what she was doing. Although
the poem is one of many, its concluding lines—with their
synesthetic figuration of nature as a housewife 'in an
Opal Apron/Mixing fresher Air'—are Dickinson at her
best: witty, immediate, precise and unique. In them, the
awesome aspects of the thunder storm ('Eclipse' and
'Awe' are terms Dickinson uses elsewhere for male
power) are converted—made nurturant as bread dough
or, perhaps, delicious as cake batter—by a woman poet's
pen.[19]
    In other poems, these same qualities of immediacy,
preciseness and wit, raise Dickinson's domesticated
'nature studies' to the level of genius:

A Route of Evanescence
With a revolving Wheel—
A Resonance of Emerald—
A Rush of Cochineal—
And every Blossom on the Bush

Adjusts it's tumbled Head—
The Mail from Tunis, probably,
An easy Morning's Ride—
(#1463, P,1010)

The technical brilliance of 'A Route of Evanescence' is so
well-documented it does not require further substantia-
tion here. With only one verb in eight lines, Dickinson
has nonetheless managed to convey a rush of pure
energy. Through paradox and synesthesia, she gives us
the essence of the ruby-throated hummingbird, the
unnamed subject of this poem, without literally describ-
ing the bird at all. What with its extraordinary syntax and
gaudy diction, especially the unexpected leap to Tunis
in the final lines (a probable reference to Shakespeare's
The Tempest [II.i.66–72]), 'A Route of Evanescence' is one
of Dickinson's most exotic—and successful—efforts.[20]
Yet what I would like to stress here is—paradoxically—
not just the accuracy but the homeliness of Dickinson's
depiction, its place, that is, within the female artistic
tradition.

'Hummingbirds,' Crawford Greenwalt writes, 'have
the highest energy output per unit of weight of any living
warm-blooded animal.'[21] With bodies averaging two to
three inches long, they are extremely difficult to see,
both because of their size and because of the peculiar
directionality as well as speed of their flight. (Unlike
other birds, hummingbirds can not only hover in place,
but fly backwards.) You are as likely to become aware of
them by the light flashing from their irridescent feathers
or by the resonance of their hum (a low buzzing caused
by the rapid beating of their wings) as by actual sighting.

As the owner of a New England flower garden, Dickin-
son did not have to travel to 'Tunis'—or to Shakespeare's
imaginary island—in order to experience this tiny crea-

ture's 'magical' mode of flight. The only member of its species native to northeast America, ruby-throats haunt our gardens in the summer. In the poem, Dickinson depicts the bird as she knew it, hoping, as she tells Helen Hunt Jackson, when sending the poem to her, that her description is 'not untrue' (L,639). It is hard to imagine how it could be truer. In leaving her hummingbird a set of flashing impressions, Dickinson has 'sketched' her subject to the life—just as by alluding to *The Tempest* she has located her experience firmly in her own backyard.

Like her need to root the sources of her nature art in the familiar, the importance of Dickinson's concern for 'truth' in this poem cannot be overestimated. Like Emily Brontë, Beatrix Potter and, indeed, her own future editor, Mabel Loomis Todd, all of whom sketched from nature, Dickinson has taken nature as her guide. As visually gifted in her way as these women artists were in theirs, her poems are verbal substitutes for the drawings she might otherwise have made. And it was, it seems, as 'drawings' that she shared them with her friends. Part of the same impulse that produced C. M. Badger's *Wild Flowers Drawn and Colored from Nature*—and *Leaf and Flower Pictures, and How to Make Them*—her poems were poems and pictures in one.

Thus, for example, when Helen Hunt Jackson, impressed by the expertise of Dickinson's bluebird poem, asked the poet for an oriole, Dickinson not only complied, but added a hummingbird for good measure (L,639), hoping, as noted, that it too was 'not untrue.' Among the many nature poems sent Susan Gilbert Dickinson, there are ten sunset poems alone. Susan's house stood west of the Homestead and, as Adalaide Morris suggests, Dickinson seems to have associated her sister-in-law with the beauties of the setting sun.[22] Of the thirty-five poems she sent to Elizabeth Holland, sixteen had flowers, birds or other common natural phenomena for their subject. To Eudocia Flint, and many others, she sent flowers with poem/notes in combination.[23]

In many of these poems or in their accompanying messages, Dickinson is specific about her intent. 'Lest she miss her "Squirrels," I send her little Playmates I met in Yesterday's Storm,' she wrote to the daughter of a woman friend in 1883, accompanying her note with a poem on robins (L,766). 'I'll tell you how the Sun rose,' poem #318 begins. In poems such as 'How the old Mountains drip with Sunset' (#291) and 'The Trees like Tassels—hit—and swung' (#606), she is even bolder, explicitly challenging the great European painters—Guido Reni, Titian, Domenichino, and Vandyke—with her own domesticated female renditions. Such statements indicate that for Dickinson, as for most women poets in this period, the poem was the verbal or symbolic representation of its subject—a 'painting' of another kind. As she says in a note sent with a flower and poem, the former sent 'a message by a Mouth that cannot speak—' (L,878). The poem was the 'message's' verbal representation. In her 'Introduction' to Badger's book, Lydia Huntley Sigourney makes a similar claim for that artist's poetic and artistic efforts:

> —One fair hand, hath skill'd to bring
> Voice of bird, and breath of Spring,
> One fair hand, before you laid
> Flowerets that can never fade,—
> While you listen, soft and clear
> Steals her wind-harp o'er your ear,—
> While you gaze, her buds grow brighter,—
> Take the book, and bless its writer.[24]

Badger accompanies her prints with poems also meant to 'represent' (or speak for) the flowers she depicts: the

Fringed Gentian, by C. M. Badger.
(Reproduced by permission of the Houghton Library,
Harvard University.)

arbutus, violet, clover, wood lily, fringed gentian, hare-
bell and rose, among others. Like Dickinson's poems on
these same flowers, Badger's poems and prints are
intimate studies (see frontispiece and the illustration on
page 101), suited to the domestic representational tradi-
tion in which both women worked, a tradition that
valued smallness and detail over the grand and often
foreign vistas favored by men.[25]

In her study of the role that detail has played in West-
ern masculinist aesthetics from the eighteenth century
on, Naomi Schor writes:

> to retell the story [of the decline of idealism] from the per-
> spective of detail is inevitably to tell *another* story. To focus
> on the detail . . . is to become aware . . . of its participation in
> a larger semantic network, bounded on the one side by the
> *ornamental*, with its traditional connotations of effeminacy
> and decadence, and on the other, by the *everyday*, whose
> 'prosiness' is rooted in the domestic sphere of social life pre-
> sided over by women. In other words, to focus on . . . detail
> . . . is to become aware that the normative aesthetics elabor-
> ated and disseminated by the Academy and its members is
> not sexually neutral; it is an axiology carrying into the field
> of representation the sexual hierarchies of the phallocentric
> cultural order. The detail does not occupy a conceptual
> space beyond the laws of sexual difference: the detail is
> gendered and doubly gendered as feminine.[26]

Schor does not discuss the differences between male and
female art. Indeed, she treats no women artists. But it is
precisely this kind of detail, bounded on one side by the
'*ornamental*' and on the other by the '*everyday*,' that
Dickinson, like other women nature poets of her period,
makes the substance of her text. In her study of landscape
in American poetry (1879), a study devoted almost exclus-
ively to male writing, Lucy Larcom calls such details 'the

homelier aspects of life and Nature,' and comments on their rarity. 'Who else,' she asks, praising Lowell's courage, 'has dared bring into poetry that plain bird, the black thrush [the catbird], whose song is both a feline mew and an entrancing carol?'[27]

Individual studies of birds, beasts and flowers are in fact relatively rare in the poetry of nineteenth-century men.[28] But they are not infrequent in the work of women poets, and they are certainly not rare in Dickinson. Not only did she write up to six poems apiece on fourteen different species of birds and fifteen different species of flowers—including the singularly 'unpoetic' jewel-weed; but she also wrote over two dozen poems on assorted other creatures as well: cats, caterpillars, spiders, worms, snakes, crickets, butterflies and fireflies. In fact, contrary to all idealizing aesthetic practices, including those of her own era, she seems to have found no creature too mean or 'homely' to focus on—not that 'concise' tenant, the rat (#1356), nor the dive-bombing June Beetle, 'terror of the Children' and 'merriment of men' (#1128, P,791 and 792). In each instance, like Sigourney with her alpine flowers, Dickinson focuses on a lowly detail—and in many of them, she, too, found images which intimated the divine:

A Bird came down the
Walk—
He did not know I saw—
He +bit an Angle Worm
in halves
And ate the fellow, raw,

And then, he drank a
Dew
From a convenient Grass—
And then hopped sidewise
to the Wall
To let a Beetle pass—

He glanced with rapid eyes
That hurried all around—
They looked like frightened
Beads, I thought,
He stirred his Velvet Head—

Like one in danger, cautious,
I offered him a Crumb,
And he unrolled his feathers,
And rowed him softer Home—

Than Oars divide the
Ocean,
Too silver for a seam,
Or Butterflies, off Banks
of Noon,
Leap, plashless as they
swim.

+shook
8(#328, F,373–4)

Whatever one wants to make of the conclusion of this poem, the first fourteen lines contain some of the most precise and highly-individualized nature description in the language. The bird is a robin. Every motion and gesture, every habit, is perfectly caught—the way the robin hops along the ground, head cocked, listening for worms; the beady, darting eyes; the way it cuts the worm with its beak and drinks dew from the grass. (Yes, robins do.) Dickinson loved robins. She referred to them as Gabriels, presumably because, as the first birds to return in spring (the act for which New Englanders cherish them), they announce the 'resurrection' (L,766). She also knew them well.

But, obviously, this poem is not just a description of a robin. In the final six lines, the robin, frightened by the speaker's attempt to give it a crumb, flies off and, I am tempted to say, the poem takes off with it. The entire quality of the writing changes, disrupting the narrative or 'prose' flow and becoming lushly analogic ('poetic') instead. Heaven is an ocean through which the bird 'rows' home. Its feathers are oars that cut more seamlessly through air than real oars cut through water silvered by light. (The shifting light on the water masks the shadow of the oars' entrance.) Taking the analogy one step further, the bird flies as soundlessly in the sky as butterflies 'swim' when they 'leap' off 'banks of noon,' that is, when they fly off into the air—or, more likely, into eternity.

At the moment of observation, when the bird takes flight, the speaker has an experience of the numinous. More at home in the sky than on earth, the bird is a messenger from heaven, the 'Home' to which it returns. Hence the lack of division between it and the element through which it 'seamlessly' passes. Bird and sky are one. Loving birds 'is economical,' Dickinson informed Eugenia Hall in 1876. 'It saves going to Heaven' (L,550).

I believe that for Dickinson such moments of revelation *were* the equivalent of experiencing heaven. And they explain, therefore, how she could make of nature an alternative religion as well as a source of poetic strength. Birds were birds, but they were also something more. *Insofar as they partook of beauty*, they, like flowers, like electric storms, like the entire natural world, down, possibly, to its most 'homely' or 'meanest' moments, were part of the numinous. That is, they were part of heaven. Apprehending their beauty, Dickinson was able to have on earth the 'Bliss' which the traditionally religious reserved only for those who were saved—and which male artists used only the 'sublime' (the ideal) to figure forth.[29] And it was from this 'Bliss,' this intense emotionally- and sensually-charged apprehension of beauty—that the lush analogies of Dickinson's poetry come. Without such revelations, paradise itself, for this poet, would have no appeal. 'The immortality of Flowers must enrich our own, and we certainly should resent a Redemption that excluded them,' Dickinson wrote to Mrs Edward Tuckerman in about 1877 (L,597).

Dickinson's famous comparison of nature to a 'Haunted House,' and art to a 'House that tries to be haunted' (L,554), must be read in this light. 'When much in the Woods as a little Girl,' the poet wrote Higginson in 1862, 'I was told that the Snake would bite me, that I might pick a poisonous flower, or Goblins kidnap me, but I went along and met no one but Angels [birds?], who were far shyer of me, than I could be of them' (L,415). If Nature were 'haunted,' the spirits ('Angels') who haunted her were good, not evil. Her witchery brought ecstasy, not death. And it was this ecstasy—at once sensuous and religious—that Dickinson reproduced in her poems.

In an extraordinary passage sent to the Norcross cousins in 1876, to thank them for a gift of witchhazel stalks, Dickinson brings these ideas together. To the poet, even a sprig of witchhazel, closely observed, can become an occasion of ecstatic 'joy,' a moment of heavenly or 'mystical' vision, that she is then compelled to set down in words:

> Oh that beloved *witch*-hazel which would not reach me till part of the stems were a gentle brown, though one loved stalk as hearty as if just placed in the mail by the woods. It looked like tinsel fringe combined with staider fringes, *witch* and *witching* too, to my *joyful* mind.

I never had seen it but once before, and it *haunted* me like
childhood's Indian pipe, or *ecstatic* puff-balls, or that *mysterious*
apple [a gall or fungus] that sometimes comes on river-pinks;
and is there not a dim suggestion of a dandelion, if her hair
were ravelled and she grew on a twig instead of a tube. . . .
For taking Nature's hand to lead her to me, I am softly grate-
ful—was she willing to come?

(L,568, my italics.)

It is precisely the combination of intense emotional and
spiritual experience with acutely detailed, materially-
based observation that makes this passage—and Dickin-
son's nature poetry as a whole—so incredibly powerful
and so peculiarly hers. The witchhazel—closely exam-
ined—becomes the axis for a ('sentimental') fantasia
upon bewitching growths: Indian pipe, puff-balls, fun-
gus galls, and dandelions.[30] For each of these is one of
childhood's mysteries and in the very uncanniness of its
beauty (a beauty that springs from the meanest of places)
represents an 'Angel' in the woods. Each is, therefore, a
potential spirit with which she can 'haunt' her house of
art and disrupt the flow of 'prose' life. Each, that is,
yields poetry—a specifically female poetry, in that it is
spiritual and sensual, domestic and be*witch*ing, humble
and strange, at once.

For Dickinson, nature's 'tinsel' was replete with such
mysteries, moments and messages and it was her task as
poet to absorb them and to give them back. To the poet,
this process of absorption and giving back was an in-
ebriating experience, for it brought her in touch with the
very wellsprings of her religious as well as her poetic
fervor, filling her with a divine afflatus any traditionally-
oriented poet might envy. But as the witch-hazel fantasia
suggests, despite its emphasis on the numinous, this
afflatus was in no way a transcendental experience.

Indeed it had nothing in common with the kind of transcendence of the material world men like Emerson yearned to enjoy:

> I taste a liquor never brewed—
> From Tankards scooped in Pearl—
> +Not all the Frankfort Berries
> Yield such an Alcohol!
>
> Inebriate of Air—am I—
> And Debauchee of Dew—
> Reeling—thro endless summer days—
> From inns of Molten Blue—
>
> When "Landlords" turn the drunken Bee
> Out of the Foxglove's door—
> When Butterflies—renounce their "drams"—
> I shall but drink the more!
>
> Till Seraphs swing their snowy Hats—
> And Saints—to windows run—
> To see the little Tippler
> +From Manzanilla come!

+vats upon the Rhine +Leaning against the—Sun—

(#214, F,227)

Dickinson drew the central figure for this poem from Emerson's essay, 'The Poet.' But as many scholars have noted, she did so to make her difference—not her debt—clear. In this essay, Emerson gives some typically Emersonian good advice. The poet, he declares, should live in such a way that the 'common influences' delight him. 'His cheerfulness should be the gift of the sunlight; the air should suffice for his inspiration, and he should be tipsy with water . . . If,' the Concord sage warns, 'thou fill thy brain with Boston and New York . . . and . . . stimulate thy jaded senses with wine and French coffee, thou shalt find no radiance of wisdom in the lonely waste of the pine woods.'[31]

As Karl Keller observes, the temperateness of Emerson's advice stands in stark contrast to Dickinson's 'raucous' celebration of her debauchery.[31] Like so much else in Emerson, it is rooted in his profound distrust of the material world. 'Poetry,' Emerson writes in another essay, 'is the perpetual endeavor to express the spirit of the thing, to pass the brute body and search the life and reason which causes it to exist—to see that the object is always flowing away, whilst the spirit or necessity which causes it subsists.'[33] In this sense, Emerson's approach to nature is indeed transcendental. It seeks to rise above matter to apprehend the 'spirit' which is, presumably, matter's cause. For Emerson, as—Barton Levi St. Armand has demonstrated—for other male theorists in his culture, the details of nature were a veil through which we are meant to perceive the spirit (or in Agassiz's case, the 'mind') of God.[34]

In 'I taste a liquor never brewed,' on the other hand, it is precisely in the immanence of nature, its 'brute' (female) materiality, that the speaker rejoices—the breath and beauty of the natural world pulsing through her senses, the look, sound and feel of life. This, according to Dickinson, was 'Bliss' and this is what her poems on nature seek to convey through the specificity of their detail and the vividness of their figures: a 'paradise' of beauty equal to God's own and a good deal more available. Despite the experience of the numinous within it, the actual transcendence of nature is the last thing that Emily Dickinson's nature poetry is about. As she says in 'I taste a liquor never brewed,' she wants to soak in individual moments of natural beauty (to become 'high' on them) to the day she dies. (The third stanza refers to late summer when bees can sometimes be seen lying sluggishly on the petals of the flowers from which they feed, and butterflies near the end of their exquisite lives.)

In 'Before I got my eye put out,' Dickinson hints that her potential for this kind of intense, affective sense experience was so great that it 'blinded' her. (That is, it frightened her into caution.)

> Before I got my eye put out
> I liked as well to see—
> As other Creatures, that have Eyes
> And know no other way—
>
> But were it told to me—Today—
> That I might have the sky
> For mine—I tell you that my Heart
> Would split, for size of me—
>
> The Meadows—mine—
> The Mountains—mine—
> All Forests—Stintless Stars—
> As much of Noon as I could take
> Between my finite eyes—
>
> The Motions of The Dipping Birds—
> The Morning's Amber Road—
> For mine—to look at when I liked—
> The News would strike me dead—
>
> So safer Guess—with just my soul
> Upon the Window pane—
> Where other Creatures put their eyes—
> Incautious—of the Sun—
>
> (#327, P,259–60. Version to T. W. Higginson.)

In letters and poems written throughout her life, Dickinson declines particular experiences on the grounds that having them would overwhelm her. Thus, in *c.* 1852, she refuses to visit Emily Fowler Ford because she would be 'so happy' she would never want to leave (L,184).

Similarly, *c.* 1878, she tells Sue that they must space their visits because seeing her sister-in-law is 'too moment-ous.' '[R]emember,' she adds, 'it is idolatry, not indiffer-ence' (L,631).

Such excuses may have been graceful ways for the in-creasingly reclusive poet to get out of having to see people; but Higginson's comment that his interview with Dickinson left him utterly drained ('I am glad not to live near her,' he said later, [L,476]), suggests that Dickin-son's mode of relating was 'too intense.' She gave out too much. And, as 'Before I got my eye put out' indicates, she took too much in: mountains, meadows, noon (here, eternity clearly). In the poem, her speaker claims that there was a time when she could 'see' such things the way other people saw them, without truly 'seeing' them, that is, in the limited two-dimensional way we have of looking at pictures. But something happened which, in effect, 'blinded' her—it was, apparently, too much, too vast, like looking at the sun—and now she is cautious where she puts her eyes, preferring to see with her 'soul' instead (that is, possibly, through the remove that poetry provides). 'Had we the first intimation of the Definition of Life, the calmest of us would be Lunatics,' Dickinson declared to Mrs Holland in 1877 (L,576).

'Before I got my eye put out' is a difficult and elusive poem. But the contrast it draws between the way Dickin-son sees and the way she believes others see seems clear. It also seems just. Even in a poem such as 'I taste a liquor never brewed,' which has a literary source and was writ-ten relatively early in her career, the difference between Dickinson's way of 'seeing' and the way others see—in this case, Emerson—could not be more striking. For Dickinson is immediate where Emerson is distant, she is visual where Emerson is vague, she is concrete where Emerson is abstract. Above all, she is full of feeling where Emerson, bound up in ratiocination, is, affectively-speaking, just about dead.

The power of 'I taste a liquor never brewed,' does not lie in the 'wisdom' the poet wants to convey (or in the sublimity she seeks to express), but in the poem's specificity and figural detail. Because of the denseness of the figurative language, the speaker's experience is grounded in sensation so that the reader feels it too. Thus the speaker does not simply enjoy 'the gift of sunlight,' she 'reels' through 'endless summer days' from 'inns' of 'Molten Blue.' She does not just get 'tipsy with water,' she speaks tankards 'scooped in pearl' and is a 'Debauchee of Dew.' Such figures are not simply decorative—nor are they derivative, part of a stale poetic vocabulary.[35] In their freshness and vividness, they convey linguistically the sensations Dickinson's speaker experienced, making us experience them too. As Dickinson told Higginson, in their meeting in 1870, ' "If I read a book [and] it makes my whole body so cold no fire ever can warm me I know *that* is poetry. If I feel physically as if the top of my head were taken off, I know *that* is poetry. These are the only way I know it. Is there any other way" ' (L,473–4).

It was this sort of explosive affective and sensual reaction Dickinson wanted, and it was this sort of explosive reaction she got. To read her poetry is to experience what she experienced as if one saw, heard and tasted with her eyes, ears and tongue. It is no wonder, then, that she described art as a 'House that tries to be haunted' or that she rebelled so fiercely at the idea of having to give the body up. To have eternity without the body, to be spirit without flesh, was in Dickinson's mind to have nothing at all, no matter what promises Christ made. It was in the flesh—in nature, in the material—that we experienced the 'Bliss' of paradise, be heaven what it will. 'Let me commend to Baby's attention the only Commandment I ever obeyed,' she wrote Mrs Tuckerman's niece after the birth of her daughter in 1884. ' "Consider the Lilies" ' (L,825). It was the only commandment Dickinson knew could assure her of the heaven she wanted, the heaven that was here and now in the 'sweet smiles and fragrance' of the wild flowers (L,66) and 'The Motions of The Dipping Birds.'

Dickinson's unique qualities as a nature poet cannot be separated from her gender or from her determination to maintain her identification with nature as female, separate from masculinist religious, philosophic and artistic traditions. Drawing heavily on the female artistic tradition which domesticated nature and found value in detail, Dickinson used the nature around her to make her art and to justify her religion. Going to her sister's garden, she discovered a world of beauty and sensation she could compress into poetry that was, *sui generis*, its own kind and irreducibly hers—a poetry in which the details of matter and the 'essence' of spirit were, finally, one:

> Essential Oils—are wrung—
> The Attar from the Rose
> Be not expressed by Suns—
> alone—
> It is the gift of Screws—
>
> The General Rose—decay—
> But this—in Lady's Drawer
> Make Summer—When the
> Lady lie
> In Ceaseless Rosemary—
> (#675, F,836)

In this, one of her most grammatically experimental

poems,[36] Dickinson asserts both the timelessness of her art and the emphemerality of all it contains. For the poet-speaker in this poem is both a compressor of essences and a maker of perfume. Essence and sensation cannot be separated from each other. Both are captured in the fleeting moment of the rose's perfume just as the perfume is captured in the poem and the poem is captured in the lady's drawer. All 'be' at once: making 'Summer—When the/Lady lie/In Ceaseless Rosemary.' One cannot be said to be ontologically prior to the other. Like the uninflected verbs in this poem, they are timeless and timebound at once.

Although in some poems Dickinson seems to suggest that it is the prerogative of art to make the present (the ephemeral, nature, femaleness, the general rose), eternal, there was no way, finally, for her to decide between the competing claims of nature and art. In some poems, as in 'I reckon—when I count at all' (#569), she makes art ontologically superior to nature, containing and superceding it. In others, however, she views her poems as 'Menagerie' (fleeting exhibitions) when compared to nature's 'Competeless Show' (#290, F,269). As in 'The Spider holds a Silver Ball,' she could not choose between two opposing points of view on her profession. Nor did her art suffer because she could not.

Dickinson's inability to choose between nature and art was rooted in her deep-seated need to find in nature an alternative source of power equal to that traditionally attributed to a transcendent God, a power that could heal the rents and tears her metaphysics made in reality and her scepticism made in the body of truth. Without nature, everything would have been illusion to this poet or—as she says so bitterly in 'Finding is the first /Act'—'sham' (#870, F,1043). She would indeed have been the 'postmodernist' that Porter and other linguistically-oriented critics have made her out to be—a deconstructionist for whom little beside words detached from transcendent meaning can be said to exist, a subjectivist living inside her own head.

But Dickinson found another path to being and truth—one that lay outside masculinist literary and religious structures and was therefore empowering to her, one whose reality, however ephemeral, she could test with her senses and reconstitute in all its mystery in her verse. Nature nurtured her. Nature was her mother. She did not have to go further than Vinnie's garden to find her. She did not need 'faded men' to tell her that the Bliss she experienced there was good.

Chapter Four

Polar Privacy

The king is surrounded by persons whose only thought is to divert the king, and to prevent his thinking of self. For he is unhappy, king though he be, if he think of himself.

(Pascal, *Pensées*)

"How do most people live without any thoughts. There are many people in the world (you must have noticed them in the street) How do they live. How do they get strength to put on their clothes in the morning"

(Dickinson as quoted by T. W. Higginson 1870)

While Dickinson's nature poetry is directed toward representations of the material world, it is also true that she employed metaphors drawn from nature to illustrate the inner life. In some poems she uses rare natural cataclysms, volcanoes and earthquakes, to express the violence and alienating effect of inwardly-withheld emotion. In others, everyday phenomena, such as the quality of light on winter afternoons or the late August song of

116

the crickets, are enlisted to evoke thoughts or feelings, shared, presumably, by us all:[1]

> There's a certain Slant of light,
> Winter Afternoons—
> That oppresses, like the Heft
> Of Cathedral Tunes—
>
> Heavenly Hurt, it gives us—
> We can find no scar,
> But internal difference,
> Where the Meanings, are—
>
> None may teach it—Any—
> 'Tis the Seal Despair—
> An imperial affliction
> Sent us of the Air—
>
> When it comes, the Landsape listens—
> Shadows—hold their breath—
> When it goes, 'tis like the Distance
> On the look of Death—
>
> (#258, F,270)

With its exquisite use of sound, its disjunctive grammar, and mixed levels of diction, 'There's a certain Slant of light' is a formidable performance. But the reason for the poem's extraordinary popularity (it is among Dickinson's most consistently reprinted and explicated works) does not lie in technique alone. It also lies in our familiarity with the experience Dickinson describes. Not only has the poet captured the oddness of winter light (its thin, estranging quality), but she has also caught the depressed or sorrowful state of mind which this light biochemically induces. Despite the poet's use of terms like 'Seal' and 'imperial affliction,' that key into her private mythology of self—her self-designated role as 'Queen of

117

Calvary'—'There's a certain Slant of light' engages its readers directly.[2]

Yet at the same time, 'There's a certain Slant of light' is, obviously, a highly subjective poem, dealing with an intensely personal state of mind. In it, the speaker's mood takes over from the light, the presumptive focus of the text, and is generalized to the entire landscape. The world becomes a partner in the poet's depression. The depression becomes the lens through which the world is seen—and, even more important, through which its 'meanings' (whatever they might be) are understood.

When Dickinson uses nature imagery in this way, she is appropriating it, as Joanne Feit Diehl says, for the 'aggrandizement of the mind.'[3] In such poems, the natural phenomenon *'becomes* the self as the division between identity and scene dissolves.'[4] To that extent, 'There's a certain Slant of light' may be said to be solipsistic. That is, unlike the nature poems discussed in the preceding chapter, it is explicitly a projection of the poet's inner life, a massive transference to the landscape of her inner state of being. Dickinson reveals the nature of this state through her comparisons, but its meaning is one she refuses to disclose. For all its apparent familiarity, what happens in this poem is, finally, as fragmented and inconclusive (as unknowable) as the light to which Dickinson refers—or the grammar she uses.

The evasiveness of 'There's a certain Slant of light'—its multiple ambiguities and its refusal to reach a firm conclusion—is typical of Dickinson's psychological poems and the source of much of their difficulty (as well as their fascination). Reading Dickinson's poetry, Adrienne Rich declares, one gets the sense 'of a mind engaged in a lifetime's musing on essential problems of language, identity, separation, relationship, the integrity of the self; a mind capable of describing psychological states

118

more accurately than any poet except Shakespeare.'[5] No poet seems closer to her readers as a result. It is as if Dickinson laid out her most private thoughts and feelings before us.

But unlike the accessibility of Dickinson's nature poetry, which is supported by the external world to which the poems refer, the accessibility of Dickinson's psychological poetry is in many ways deceiving. Not only is the relationship between the voice which speaks these poems and Dickinson herself problematic, but so, as a rule, is the relationship between the poetry's manifest content and the meaning which this content presumably encodes. Thus, on the most basic level, it is unclear whether Dickinson addresses her own feelings in 'There's a certain Slant of light,' or those she believes are people's in general, and we may query whether the poem is about light or about the depression which the light evokes. Finally, we may ask what 'meaning' this light (or this depression) has, especially given its status as an 'imperial affliction/Sent us,' we are told, 'of the Air.' This chapter will discuss the difficulties involved in reading Dickinson's psychological poems and the ramifications these difficulties have for our understanding of the relationship between the poet's life and her work. Like other nineteenth-century women poets, Dickinson used her poetry to inscribe her 'heart's record,'[6] but the ambiguities of her technique and the complexity and richness of her inscription make the interpretation of this record a subject of intense (and at times, perhaps, futile) critical debate.

In poems written throughout her life, Dickinson describes inquiry into self as an exhilarating but highly dangerous imperative.[7] Death might be the 'undiscovered country, from whose bourn/No traveller returns,' but to Dickinson, the human soul constituted a site of equally risky, if necessary, exploration. In 'Soto! Explore thyself!'—a poem which she sent to Austin, interestingly enough—the soul is the '"Undiscovered Continent"' we are obliged to study first (#832, F,1059). In 'There is a solitude of space,' it is a 'polar privacy' (#1695, P,1149). When entering this privacy, the speaker not only cuts herself off from other forms of human interaction, she also confronts matter most people wish only to avoid:

> Its' Hour with
> itself
> The Spirit never
> shows.
> What Terror would
> enthrall the Street
> Could Countenance
> disclose
>
> The Subterranean
> Freight
> The Cellars of
> the Soul—
> Thank God the
> loudest Place he
> made
> Is licensed to be
> still.
> (#1225, F,1277)

There were, Dickinson knew, discoveries no one should reveal.

If Dickinson were aware of the dangers inherent in self-examination, however, this knowledge does not seem to have deterred her. Indeed, if anything, she appears to have organized her life in such a way as to give maximum scope to this inquiry. Confined to life 'at home' in any case, she turned her privacy into the ground on which her discoveries were made. Her principal occupations: sewing, baking and gardening, allowed plenty of time for rumination. She intensified her isolation by allowing few outside visitors or events to distract her from her pursuit. As she declares in 'This Consciousness that /is aware,' self-exploration was a task that had to be performed alone, and she seems to have stripped her own life accordingly. Unlike Pascal's king, this Queen of None wanted no diversions:

This Consciousness that
is aware
Of Neighbors and the Sun
Will be the one aware
of Death
And that itself alone

Is traversing the interval
Experience between
And most profound
experiment
Appointed unto Men—

How adequate unto itself
It's properties shall be
Itself unto itself and none
Shall make discovery—

Adventure most unto
itself
The Soul condemned to be—
Attended by a single
Hound
It's own identity.
                    (#822, F,1085–6)

As Karl Keller has observed, there is a kind of old-fashioned, bravura Puritanism in the stance Dickinson's speaker assumes in such a poem.[8] The poet appears to be carrying the original Puritan injunction to examine closely the state of one's soul as far as it will go. Abjuring all props in the pursuit of her goal—including, most significantly, the fellowship and guidance offered by the church—her speaker relies on the 'properties' of the self instead. Whether or not these properties turn out to be adequate is, the speaker claims, only for herself and the Lord to know. Of her desire to shun '"Men and Women",' Dickinson wrote to Higginson in 1862, 'they talk of Hallowed things, aloud—and embarrass my Dog—He and I dont object to them, if they'll exist their side' (L,415). Like Milton, Dickinson seems to be moving toward a religion of one.

In fact, however, Dickinson was not moving toward a 'religion' at all. Although she employs terms like 'Soul' and speaks of an 'experiment' that has been 'Appointed' and of 'Hallowed things,' the aim of this poem, as of Dickinson's poems on self-examination generally, was not to achieve a state of grace in God's eyes—the Puritan goal. If anything, it was to celebrate the survival of the soul under the adverse conditions which God had appointed for it. Dickinson studied the soul not to prepare it for divine mercy, but because she loved it. And she wondered over and over again at its enormous power to endure, indeed to transcend, the pounding that life—or God—gave it.

A poem such as 'Dare you see a Soul *at the White Heat*' will illustrate what I mean. At the same time, it will help establish the central role that evasiveness—or ambiguity—plays in Dickinson's technique:

Polar Privacy

Dare you see a Soul *at the White Heat*?
Then crouch within the door—
Red—is the Fire's common tint—
But when the vivid Ore
Has vanquished Flame's conditions,
It quivers from the Forge
Without a color, but the light
Of unannointed Blaze.
Least Village has it's Blacksmith
Whose Anvil's even ring
Stands symbol for the finer Forge
That soundless tugs—within—
Refining these impatient Ores
With Hammer, and with Blaze
Until the Designated Light
Repudiate the Forge—

(#365, P,289–90)

At first glance, 'Dare you see a Soul *at the White Heat*'
looks like a fairly traditional rendering of the soul's test-
ing, but it is not. To appreciate how deviant this poem is
one need only compare it to a more traditional treatment
of the same subject matter—for example, Anne Brad-
street's theocentric version of the soul's trials in 'For
Deliverance from a Fever':

When sorrows had begirt me round,
And pains within and out,
When in my flesh no part was found,
Then didst Thou rid me out.
My burning flesh in sweat did boil,
My aching head did break,
. . . . .
"Hide not Thy face from me!" I cried,
"From burnings keep my soul.
Thou know'st my heart, and hast me tried;
I on Thy mercies roll."

123

"O heal my soul," Thou know'st I said,
"Though flesh consume to nought,
What though in dust it shall be laid,
To glory t'shall be brought."
Thou heard'st, Thy rod Thou didst remove
And spared my body frail,
Thou show'st to me Thy tender love,
My heart no more might quail
O, praises to my mighty God,
Praise to my Lord, I say,
Who hath redeemed my soul from pit,
Praises to Him for aye. [9]

Whatever one wants to say about the subject of Brad-
street's poem, it is not ambiguous. On the contrary. The
significance of the fever episode is established both in the
speaker's mind and in ours. It is a type for the working
out of the soul's redemption. God burns away the flesh
and, through that burning, heals the soul, preparing it to
receive the tenderness of divine grace. Indeed, Bradstreet
depicts the entire episode as part of the 'testing' proced-
ure by which God makes the penitent fit to receive His
mercy. And, according to Wendy Martin, this is precisely
how Bradstreet, like other Puritans, did view the afflic-
tions which God sent with such great regularity. Seen
in this perspective, Martin comments, 'paradoxically suf-
fering was a form of joy,' a cause for celebration. [10]

In Dickinson, too, the 'White Heat' of suffering appears
paradoxically to benefit the soul, but that is where the
similarity between her poem and Bradstreet's ends. For
Dickinson's concern is not with preparing her soul to
receive grace. It is with describing the way in which the
soul is empowered through its capacity to survive and
transcend pain. Thus the blaze in her poem is 'un-
annointed;' the 'Blacksmith' is 'within.' If God exists, He
stands outside this poem and this process and He is,

arguably, irrelevant to it. As far as we are told, the transaction is entirely between the soul and its own experience, an experience which 'redeems' it, but only, it seems, in a secular sense.

The absence of an explanatory Christian framework in 'Dare you see a Soul' is crucial. Despite its Puritanical penumbra, this is in many ways a quintessentially modern poem. By refusing to employ a Christian framework to surround the idea of redemptive suffering and stabilize its meaning, indeed, in refusing even to pay lip service to this framework, Dickinson has cut her poem—and her experience—loose from the past. Without God (or some alternative philosophical ideology) to contain the poem's symbolism, 'Dare you see a Soul,' like so many modern works of art (Wallace Stevens's 'Anecdote of the Jar,' for example), becomes an ambiguous or indeterminate structure. That is, it is a metaphorical statement about experience to which any of a variety of interpretations, religious or otherwise, might apply.

The importance of this fact cannot be overestimated. 'Dare you see a Soul' may be 'about' the soul, but the soul in this case could stand for the speaker's artistic talent, her sense of self, her passion, or, indeed, any kind of internally felt power burning within her. In the same way, the blacksmith could stand for God, or life, or the speaker herself, pounding her being, her essence, into shape. Even the conclusion of the poem is ambiguous: Is it a reference to immortality? to completion? to success? Completion of what? Success at what? Is it about death? These questions haunt, but within the terms provided by the poem, they cannot be answered. And because they cannot be answered, we are forced to relate to Dickinson's poem in a new way—a way which in its openness to a multiplicity of conflicting readings is distinctly modern.[11]

This being said, however, it is also important to note that we respond emotionally to 'Dare you see a Soul' with a clarity that most postmodernist poetry does not allow. The significance of the suffering which Dickinson describes in this poem may be ambiguous and prone to slippage, but the psychological process itelf—the process of 'redemptive' suffering, suffering that strengthens—is another matter. Whatever terms we use to describe it, this is a process that our culture has consistently valorized over time. Puritans rationalized redemptive suffering under the rubric of preparation, and viewed it as part of the testing necessary to receive God's grace. In the nineteenth century, suffering was the basis upon which one learned to have 'confidence in heaven'—as Emma Embury put it, 'though thus of all bereft' (May 229). Recent psychologies have rationalized it in more secular ways: 'no pain, no gain,' for example, and the concept of 'necessary loss.'

To appreciate Dickinson's achievement in a poem such as 'Dare you see a Soul,' the importance of our familiarity with the psychological dynamic it describes *also* cannot be overestimated. Whether we want to believe that it is God who 'is' the blacksmith, or the poet's ambition, or life's sufferings internalized, we 'know' the kind of refinement through pain Dickinson's speaker depicts in this poem, just as we know, for example, the effect of winter light depicted in 'There's a certain Slant of light.' Despite its ambiguity or, rather, despite *and* because of it, the speaker's suffering (and therefore Dickinson's poem) is recognizable. Insofar as we too attribute value to suffering, it is our own. The same cannot be said with any certainty of the experience described in poems such as Stevens's 'Anecdote of the Jar.' Although there are times (e.g. in 'Four Trees—upon a solitary / Acre') when Dickinson herself appears to voice this concern—in a Dickinson poem, meaning is not lost or dispersed through the use of indeterminacy. Given her poetry's place within a shared cultural context, the multiplicity of possible interpretations only enriches our reading of it.

This same kind of description in a vacuum (that is, outside an established framework for interpretation) is typical of an astonishingly large number of Dickinson's psychological poems, and accounts in great measure for their appeal. Despite their specificity—for Dickinson is no less acute observing the soul than observing nature— the experiences in these poems cannot be pinned down to the poet's life or to a single interpretation of their meaning. On the contrary, because the poems are specific and indeterminate at once, they mirror the particular experience they describe in ways that make it generally relevant to her readers.[12] That Dickinson wanted her psychological poems to function in this way appears clear from statements that she makes in one of her longest and most revealing poems, 'I measure every Grief/I meet.' Because of the light this poem sheds on Dickinson's way of thinking and writing, I quote it in full.

I measure every Grief
I meet +analytic eyes—
With +narrow, probing, Eyes—
I wonder if It weighs
like Mine—
Or has an Easier size.

I wonder if They bore it long—
Or did it just begin—
I could not tell the Date
of Mine—
It feels so old a pain—

Emily Dickinson: Woman poet

I wonder if it hurts to live—
And if They have to try—
And whether—could They—
choose between—
It would not be—to die—

I note that Some—gone
patient long—
At length, renew their smile—
An imitation of a Light
That has so little Oil—

I wonder if when Years
have piled—
Some Thousands—on the Harm—
That hurt them early—
such a lapse
Could give them any Balm—

Or would they go on
aching still
Through Centuries of Nerve—
Enlightened to a larger Pain—
In Contrast with the Love—

The Grieved—are many—
I am told—
There is the various Cause—
Death—is but one—
And comes but once—
And only nails the Eyes—

There's Grief of Want—and
Grief of Cold—
A sort they call "Despair"—
There's Banishment from
native Eyes—
In sight of Native Air—

And though I may not
guess the kind—
Correctly—yet to me
A piercing Comfort it
affords
In passing Calvary—

To note the fashions—of the
Cross—
And how they're mostly worn—
Still fascinated to presume
That Some—are like My Own—

(#561, F,619–22)

In his introduction to *The Years and Hours of Emily
Dickinson*, Jay Leyda comments on Dickinson's penchant
for riddling structures: her tendency to omit the center,
'the circumstance too well known to be repeated' which
she deliberately leaves out.[13] Dickinson uses this tech-
nique frequently in her letters when quoting from well-
known authors or from the Bible. Depending on her re-
spondent's knowledge of the passage to fill in the missing
text, she omits the key line that gives her allusion point.
In *Years and Hours*, Leyda argues that Dickinson creates
similar riddles in her poems. That is, she leaves out key
pieces of information, in particular the cause(s) for the
specific emotional experiences she describes. Thus, for
example, in the poem just cited, Dickinson's speaker
wonders at length about every conceivable aspect of
other people's crosses; yet in ten stanzas never once
mentions the 'cause' of *her own* suffering—despite her
claim that it is her suffering that motivates her to take an
interest in what other people feel. We are, in other words,
being teased.

Shrewd as Leyda's insight is, however, in some ways
it is also misleading. Dickinson did omit important pieces

of information in her poems as in her letters. But in her poetry it appears that this was less because she wanted us to guess the answer than because providing a center (whether or not from her own biography) would have restricted her poem's meaning and thus reduced the range of applicability it could have. As 'I measure every Grief/I meet' indicates, to Dickinson a cause was a cause was a cause. Whether it was death, want, cold, despair or banishment (literal or figurative), that produced the individual's grief, what mattered was the suffering itself—'the fashions—of the Cross.'[14] It is this she weighs 'With narrow, probing, Eyes,' in, presumably, herself and others. She wants to know what the suffering feels like, how long it has been borne, what effect it has, how the victim responds to it, whether or not she (or he) finds it easier to bear after a long time, and so forth. Only at the very end of the poem, does the speaker acknowledge that cause is significant, and then it is only one more subject for speculation—albeit an intriguing and, perhaps, even a peculiarly comforting one.

If, as Leyda observes, Dickinson's poems 'are among the most intensely personal and yet *im*personal on record,' this is why.[15] And since Dickinson appears to ask these questions most assiduously only of herself (that is, since—despite her comment to Higginson—she presents herself as the primary speaker of these poems, the 'I'), they result in some of the finest introspective poetry in the language.[16] Dickinson (or her speaker) knew her Cross well. She studied it from every angle, studied it with the same 'objectivity,' the same accuracy, with which she studied the natural world:

Polar Privacy

It was not Death, for
I stood up,
And all the Dead, lie down—
It was not Night, for
All the Bells
Put out their Tongues, for Noon.

It was not Frost, for on
my +Flesh   +Knees
I felt Siroccos—crawl—
Nor Fire—for just my+
Marble feet   +two
Could keep a Chancel, cool—

And yet, it tasted, like
them all,
The Figures I have seen
Set orderly, for Burial,
Reminded me, of mine—

As if my life were shaven,
And fitted to a frame,
And could not breathe
without a key,
And 'twas like Midnight,
some—

When Everything that ticked—
has stopped—
And Space stares—all around—
Or Grisly frosts—first Au-
tumn morns,
Repeal the Beating Ground—

But, most, like Chaos—
Stopless—cool—
Without a Chance, or Spar—
Or even a Report of Land—
To Justify—Despair.

(#510, F,367–8)

131

In this poem Dickinson is describing a state of mind (death-in-life) that comes, as she says in a companion poem, 'After great pain' (#341). Whatever the cause for this pain (whether loss or death or any of the other reasons alluded to in 'I measure every Grief/I meet'), the sequelae are the same. Unable to handle the intensity of her suffering, the afflicted individual goes numb. Her defense system takes over, so that emotionally-speaking she feels 'dead.' Put another way, as a result of the massive suppression of effect, her life is emptied out. As she says in the final stanza, she is so indifferent, she cannot even justify 'Despair.'

What sets Dickinson's description of this state of mind apart is not the extremity of the pain she depicts (to feel 'dead' is to feel dead), but the accuracy, vividness and immediacy with which she records it. As with her nature poetry, Dickinson has 'seen' more than most of us see, and her gift with language has enabled her to describe what she sees precisely, giving us its 'Essential Oil,' its 'amazing sense' (#448, F,465).

Stanza by stanza, image by image, paradox by paradox, 'It was not Death' rings true. 'Death-in-life' is a state of internal contradiction, and it is through contradictions that Dickinson reconstructs it. Piling up one negation upon another, the speaker predicates what cannot be, of a state that nevertheless is, making her body the vehicle through which these paradoxical tensions are expressed. Thus she is dead but still stands up; 'Siroccos—crawl' across her flesh but her 'Marble feet/ Could keep a Chancel, cool.' Like a body 'Set orderly, for Burial,' she is shaved 'And fitted to a frame.' She cannot 'breathe/without a key' (presumably a clock key). These images do not simply describe. They tell us what this particular state of mind *feels* like. Ideally, because they are kinesthetic (because they are located in the body), they make us feel it too.

Once again, in other words, as in the nature poetry, the simultaneous reflection and elicitation of effect is, finally, what Dickinson's poetry is about. She wants to make us feel so cold no fire will ever warm us, as if physically the top of our heads had been taken off, not only by describing what she sees but by making us experience it too. Omitting the center (the cause) in such a case is not a deficit but one of the poem's great strengths. For it allows us to identify with the speaker's feelings whether or not we share their cause. And it is one of the principal reasons why we tend to believe, as Archibald Macleish observes, that Dickinson is talking directly to us.[17] As with her syntax, which we are forced to fill out in order to make sense of her poems, here again, we are forced to participate in the poem, to help create it, this time through our identification with the feelings it describes. We are forced, in short, to become one with the poem. Through the combined effect of projection and identification, we make it our mirror.

Poems like 'It was not Death' and 'I measure every Grief' recur again and again in the Dickinson canon and many are among her best-known and most frequently anthologized works: 'I felt a Funeral, in my Brain' (#280), 'I should have been too glad, I see' (#313), 'After great pain, a formal feeling comes' (#341), 'I dreaded that first Robin, so' (#348), 'The first Day's Night had come' (#410), 'I tie my Hat—I crease my Shawl' (#443), 'The Soul has Bandaged moments' (#512), 'From Blank to Blank' (#761), 'I felt a Cleaving in my Mind' (#937), to name only the most familiar. Whatever the event(s) behind these poems—whether a broken love affair or some other trauma (the hypotheses are rife), or, indeed, no 'event' at all save the poet's decision to write them—Dickinson clearly wished to separate them from their origin in her life. Love or any number of different experiences, including experiences based on her reading, might give rise to her emotions, but the emotions themselves are the subject on which she writes.[18] The emotions *are* the center. And however much our curiosity is piqued by the vividness with which Dickinson depicts her feelings, we do not need to know their cause for the poems to affect us. Indeed, in so far as knowing the 'cause' would restrict our reading of the poems, it is the one piece of information we can probably best do without.

But in withholding cause, Dickinson has singularly exacerbated one of the most vexing problems confronting readers of her work, namely, determining its biographical relevance, if any. I would now like to turn to this problem in order to place it within the context of Dickinson's situation as a nineteenth-century woman poet. While this perspective will not resolve specific questions regarding the relationship between individual poems and events in Dickinson's life—on the whole, such questions can never be answered—it will help ground the poems in the poet's psychological development.[19] In doing so, it will also help clarify one of the principal differences between Dickinson and other American women poets of her day.

As Cheryl Walker and Mary Kelley have shown, the demands put on American women writers in the nineteenth century were singularly contradictory. On the one hand, as women, they were supposed to live private (domestic) lives. On the other hand, their 'privacy' was what they were supposed to write about. According to Kelley, this was their 'heart's record.' 'The heart's record,' she declares in her study of nineteenth-century domestic novelists, *Private Woman, Public Stage,* was the woman's revealed record of her life of domesticity, the only life she could have. . . . She is, by default, the empress of heart. And just as the woman is only nominally a writer, her tale is only superficially imaginary. What she relates is not a literal transcription of her domestic life but its inner truth . . . the tone, the temper, the character of that life.[20]

If such expectations held true for female domestic novelists, they were even more rigidly imposed on women poets. Of the categorical distinctions dividing men and women and male and female poetry in this period, Cheryl Walker writes, 'Men think, women feel. The male poet describes "all forms of intellectual trial and conflict". . . . The female poetic sensibility equates the strings of the lyre with heartstrings.'[21] Whether her ostensible topic was religious, social or drawn from nature, effect was the woman poet's *métier*, the area in which she was freest, presumably, to excel.

But at the same time there were many emotions and desires (chief among them, anger, sexual passion and ambition), which, according to the doctrine of the day, 'good' women were not supposed to feel—just as there were others—'warm domestic affections'—to which they were supposed to devote their lives. And this contradiction inevitably had a pervasively dampening effect on women's poetry. At once free and not free to express themselves, like the mythical Philomela, whose story, Walker argues, provided the type for the woman poet in this period, nineteenth-century American women poets wove into their texts the hidden messages they could not say out loud. 'The deeper and less accessible script,' Walker writes, 'points to the part of the self that has been violated, almost rubbed out, but that speaks nevertheless. Twain's voluble poetess is consistent with an aesthetic of silence and the voice of the shuttle after all.'[22] As her persistent use of the first person singular suggests, like her fellow women writers, Dickinson also seems to have viewed her poetry—at least her psychological poetry—as her 'heart's record,' the 'inner truth' of a domestic life. This is the genre within which she is writing and, as Walker has so ably demonstrated, she employs many of the same themes and images her fellow women poets use. But Dickinson took up these themes with a difference. As Adrienne Rich asserts, for Dickinson the closed door (the totally private life) *was* freedom, and this vitally distinguishes her from other women poets of her day. Unhampered both by the pressures of publishing and, it seems, by internalized constraints, Dickinson wrote as she pleased. The difference was one between writers who—consciously or not—sacrificed their freedom to propriety and, possibly, their desire to publish, and a poet who, by embracing total domestic privacy and *not publishing*, ironically made herself free.

Dickinson's handling of the 'free-bird' poem in contrast to a more conventional treatment of this favorite woman's theme will illustrate what I mean. Here is Elizabeth Oakes-Smith, in lines quoted by Walker, on the 'free-bird':

> A simple thing, yet chancing as it did
> When life was bright with its illusive dreams,
> A pledge and promise seemed beneath it hid;
> The ocean lay before me, tinged with beams
> That lingering draped the west, a wavering stir,
> And at my feet down fell a worn, gray quill;
> An eagle, high above the darkling fir,
> . . . . .
> O noble bird! why didst thou loose for me
> Thy eagle plume? still unessayed, unknown
> Must be that pathway fearless winged by thee;
> I ask it not, no lofty flight be mine,
> I would not soar like thee, in loneliness to pine.[23]

And here is Dickinson on the same idea:

> They shut me up in Prose—
> As when a little Girl
> They put me in the Closet—
> Because they liked me "still"—
>
> Still! Could themself have peeped—
> And seen my Brain—go round—
> They might as wise have lodged a Bird
> For Treason—in the Pound—
>
> Himself has but to will
> And easy as a Star
> +Look down upon Captivity—
> And laugh—No more have I—
>
> +Abolish his—
>
> (#613, F,464)

What is striking in Oakes-Smith's poem is the degree to which the speaker depicts herself as complicit in her own defeat. Forced to choose between opposites she believes are irreconcilable—freedom and acceptance, daring and love—the speaker voluntarily gives up power and restrains her flight. Not for her, she claims, the 'lofty' path the eagle 'fearless' takes. Fear of loneliness keeps her pinned to the ground. If her woman's condition is a prison to this poet, the desire for free flight is an 'illusion' from which she turns in the end. The 'pledge' and 'promise' come to nothing. The identification between speaker and bird is broken. She will never fly (live? write?) in this way.

In Dickinson's poem the reverse occurs. The identification between speaker and bird is maintained and the prison proves to be the illusion. The attempt to shut her up in 'Prose' (the 'prose' life of duty-bound womanhood which gives rise to what Walker calls an 'aesthetic of silence'),[24] is no more effective and no more 'wise' than

137

trying to hold a bird in the pound. The brain remains free. It is physically and intellectually unimpeded and, therefore, the speaker cannot be 'stilled.' Her power to articulate remains her own. She does not abandon it nor does she submit it to prevailing cultural beliefs. To Dickinson, if we are to credit this poem, the choice (between silence and speech, imprisonment and freedom) was a matter of 'will.'[25]

Whether other women poets could in fact have 'willed' differently than they did is, at the very least, moot. There were social and personal factors that made their choices difficult, if not impossible. Theirs was an anguishing situation. But it was not Dickinson's situation. By giving up so much that these other women writers had—whether or not they wanted it—marriage, children, acceptance, a public career, Dickinson obtained the one thing they lacked, freedom. Nowhere, I would suggest, is this freedom more evident than in the psychological authenticity (the 'heart's record') of her work.

In *The Drama of the Gifted Child*, the Swiss psychoanalyst, Alice Miller, observes that limitation of emotional range is one of the hallmarks of a 'false self.'[26] Raised to believe that certain emotions and desires (anger, need, passion, pride, ambition, greed, etc.) are unacceptable or even dangerous, children who develop false selves learn to suppress large segments of their emotional potential. On a conscious level, at least, it is as if these emotions did not exist. The void created by their absence is filled instead, Miller claims, by a pervasive sense of melancholy or depression. As Walker's study suggests, it is just this sort of melancholy or depression that characterizes the work of most American women poets in Dickinson's day. Unable to separate themselves from the cultural construction of their role, even when they questioned its effect, these women did not have direct access to their feelings—with their desire, as in the Oakes-Smith poem, to 'fly.' And because they did not, they exhibit what Walker calls a 'shaky sense of subjectivity.'[27] Despite their, in some ways, formidable influence on public and private life, they could not see the nature of their internal oppression clearly. They only knew such freedom as they had was not enough and this vague, amorphous discontent saturates their work, depressing their spirit and limiting their emotional range. '[T]hese women,' Walker writes, 'established a tradition in women's poetry, a tradition embodying a particular attitude toward their lives—a frustrated, renunciatory, fantasizing, conciliatory posture. In their poetry we can still hear their dissatisfaction, even a century or more later.'[28] It is the dissatisfaction of women who, in identifying with the cultural 'truths' they purveyed, were forced to deny—or conceal from conscious awareness—the truths hidden within their selves.

While Dickinson also has her 'frustrated, renunciatory, fantasizing, [and] conciliatory' moments, the emotional range of her psychological poetry and the specificity of her moods and responses, when taken in contrast to those of other women poets (or indeed male poets) of her period, could not be more striking. Despite her ambiguity, Dickinson's depictions of emotional states are never vague nor was she afraid of extremes or contradictions. She writes about her feelings. Her feelings are almost painfully clear. They reflect the substance of her domestic condition—in Kelley's words—the 'tone and temper' of a private life, revealing both its privations and its fullness and joy.

Thus in one poem, Dickinson depicts with absurdist irony a self so convinced of its deprivation it cannot even kill itself; it lacks the power—or 'Art.'

It would have starved a Gnat—
To +live so small as I—
And yet I was a living Child—
With—Food's necessity

Upon me—like a Claw—
I could no more remove
Than I could+ coax a Leech
away—
Or make a dragon—move—

Nor like the Gnat—had I—
The privilege to fly
And +seek a Dinner for myself—
How mightier He—than I!

Nor like Himself—the Art
Upon the Window Pane
To gad my little Being out—
And not begin—again—

+dine   +modify   +gain
(#612, F,463)

While in another poem, written at or about the same time, the speaker rejoices just as hyperbolically in the permanence and wealth of all she owns:

Mine—by the Right of
the White Election!
Mine—by the Royal Seal!
Mine—by the Sign in
the Scarlet prison—
+Bars—cannot conceal!

Mine—here—in Vision—and
in Veto!
Mine—by the Grave's Repeal—
Title—Confirmed—
+Delirious Charter!
Mine—+long as Ages steal!

+Good affidavit—   +while
+Bolts

(#528, F,452)

This is no gnat. This is a Queen. Her state is not one of deprivation but of delirium. She is, if anything, too full. If 'It would have starved a Gnat' is a poem of psychological starvation, suggesting the speaker's similarity to other women in her period, 'Mine—by the Right of/the White Election' is its opposite, a poem of psychological excess, and suggests that Dickinson (or her speaker) was able, imaginatively at any rate, to transcend the limitations of her time and place. As Suzanne Juhasz has observed, for Dickinson both emotional states were, in fact, aspects of her situation (as woman and woman poet) and she was not above having her speaker play ironically on the gulf that existed between them:[29]

A Mien to move a Queen—
Half Child—Half Heroine—
An Orleans in the Eye
That puts it's manner by
For Humbler Company
When none are near
Even a Tear—
It's frequent Visitor—

A Bonnet like a Duke—
And yet a Wren's Peruke
Were not so shy
Of Goer by—

And Hands—so slight—
They would elate a sprite
With Merriment—

A Voice that Alters—Low
                    doth
And on the Ear can go
Like Let of Snow—
Or shift supreme—
As tone of Realm
On subjects Diadem—

Too small—to fear—
Too distant—to endear—
And so Men Compromise—
And just—revere—

And Men—too Brigadier—
                    (#283, F,201–2)

Child and heroine, Duke and wren, low and supreme, small and great, powerless and divinely self-empowered, Dickinson's speaker is each of these and all of them at once. The poems on Queenship, the 'White Election,' do not invalidate the poems on deprivation any more than the poems on deprivation invalidate those on her wealth. They must be taken together since the poet's deprivation (as she construed it) was, finally, the enabling condition of her art, just as her prison 'was' freedom:

To own the Art within
the Soul
The Soul to entertain
With Silence as a Company
And Festival maintain

Is an unfurnished Circumstance
Possession is to One
As an estate perpetual
Or a reduceless Mine.

(#855, F,1131)

In the 'unfurnished Circumstance' of her soul, Dickinson discovered an 'Estate perpetual.' For her, poverty was wealth as much as wealth was poverty. Being a woman and artist partook of both. One did not cancel the other out.

Like grief and joy, and imprisonment and freedom, the states of deprivation and excess were both familiar to Dickinson and both provided material for her art. She explores what it means to lack and to own in exactly the same way that she explores all other inward states, scrutinizing them carefully, weighing their paradoxes one against the other, finding metaphors to make us feel them too. As in every area she touched, these scrutinies could result in poetry that because of its very multiplicity of possible meanings, we tend to categorize as 'great':

I had been hungry, all the
Years—
My Noon had Come—to dine—
I trembling drew the Table near—
And touched the Curious Wine—

'Twas this on Tables I had
seen—
When turning, hungry, Home
I looked in Windows, for the
+Wealth
I could not hope—+for Mine—
I did not know the ample

143

Bread—
'Twas so unlike the Crumb
The Birds and I, had often
shared
In Nature's—Dining Room—

The Plenty hurt me—'Twas so
new—
Myself felt ill—and odd—
As Berry—of a Mountain Bush—
Transplanted—to the Road—

Nor was I hungry—so I
found
That Hunger—was a way
Of +Persons outside Windows—
The Entering—takes away—

+Things   +to earn   +Creatures—
(#579, F, 331-2)

There is a dreamlike quality to the setting and action in this poem that puts it in a class by itself. Taken together with the rich, overdetermined imagery (drawn, as I shall discuss in the next chapter, from erotic as well as religious vocabularies), this quality helps create a poem that seems to extend beyond the author's unconscious mind into our unconscious as well. Familiar though the experience it describes is, the poem itself is not accessible to us. We know what it is like to hunger. We know what it is like not to feel entitled to what others have. Finally, we know what it is like no longer to want—precisely because we can have. But none of this knowledge helps explain what happens in this poem. Or rather, none of it helps explain the uncanny quality that makes this poem so effective. Setting off reverberations we cannot explain, 'I had been hungry, all the/Years' seems to—and may well—come

144

from the author's dream life. We read it as a dream—and let its potential meanings, the meanings embedded in its rich, overdetermined imagery, sink through us, without ever pinning them down.

Dickinson understood deprivation and excess as she understood joy, loss and pain because she allowed herself to imagine these states of mind fully. Like her talent with words, her inner life was a 'reduceless' mine, from which she drew matter for a lifetime, as well as a polar region she felt compelled to explore. To read her poetry is to discover the many facets of this infinitely rich inner life. The moments of psychic fragmentation and tearing apart:

I felt a Cleaving in
my Mind—
As if my Brain had
split—
I tried to match it—
Seam by Seam—
But could not make
them fit—

The thought behind, I
+strove to join
Unto the thought before—
But Sequence ravelled
out of +Sound—
Like Balls—upon a
Floor—

+tried   +reach
(#937, F,1012)

Emily Dickinson: Woman poet

The suppressed rage that led her, like a number of other nineteenth-century women,[30] to write of volcanoes and earthquakes again and again:

> When Etna basks and purrs
> Naples is more afraid
> Than when she shows her Garnet Tooth—
> Security is loud—
>
> (#1146, P,803)

The terror only those willing to confront the self can know:

> One need not be a Chamber—to be Haunted—
> One need not be a House—
> The Brain—has Corridors—surpassing
> Material Place—
>
> Far safer, of a Midnight Meeting
> External Ghost
> Than it's Interior Confronting—
> That Cooler Host.
>
> (from #670, P,516–17. Version to Sue.)

And finally, the exultation she experienced, perhaps, at her own success, a 'free bird' indeed:

> She staked her +Feathers—
> Gained an Arc—
> Debated—Rose again—
> This time—beyond the
> +estimate
> Of Envy, or of Men—

And now, among
Circumference—
Her steady Boat be
seen—
At +home—among the
Billows—As
The Bough where she
was born—

+Wings—and gained a
Bush—   +inference   +ease
(#798, F,932)

Like Shakespeare's Richard II alone in his cell, Dickinson
made her brain the 'female to [her] soul' and populated
her world with 'humors' or characters drawn from her
own feelings and imagination, thus playing 'in one
person' many parts (V.v.5–10). Each of these poems
expresses at least one 'part' Dickinson 'played.' Yet they
are all parts that each of us plays or could play in a
lifetime, had we the kind of access to our emotions that
she had to hers and the kind of imagination that would
allow us to act them out fully.

It is no wonder then that Dickinson speaks of her self
in terms of paradoxes such as 'Finite Infinity' (#1695,
P,1149) and a 'reduceless Mine' (with its typically Dickin-
sonian pun). No area of her life yielded more varied mat-
ter for her pen than the soul she so devotedly examined.
As she declares in 'Drama's Vitallest Expression/is the
Common Day,' the 'Human Heart' is the 'Only Theatre
recorded/Owner cannot shut:'

Other Tragedy

Perish in the Recitation—
This—the +best enact
When the Audience is

147

scattered
And the Boxes shut—

+more exert
(from #741, F,901–2)

To Dickinson, Hamlet and Romeo were alive and well in the parts we play within ourselves.

Many critics have, understandably, seen in the emotional diversity and contradictions of Dickinson's poetry evidence of psychic fragmentation. But the various psychological states which Dickinson describes in her poetry are all ones that, in one way or another, most people experience in their lives. It is not her experience of them but the precision and vividness with which she records them that sets Dickinson apart. The split brain of 'I felt a Cleaving in my Mind,' the 'Garnet Tooth' of 'When Etna basks and purrs,' the surrealistic 'Corridors' of the Brain in 'One need not be a Chamber,' the poet-bird who stakes 'her Feathers' and gains 'an Arc,' are all images that stun. They force us into an intense awareness of the states they describe, states that we ourselves are likely to suppress or at the very least to dampen. How, we wonder, could any person remain sane and still feel so diversely and at such a pitch.

Yet it was precisely because she did have such full access to these (sometimes 'dangerous') emotions that Dickinson remained sane. Her energy was not bound up in repression. She knew clearly who and what she was. In striking contrast to the 'shaky sense of subjectivity' other American women poets in her period exhibit, Dickinson's sense of self was utterly firm. According to her speaker, it was also self-sufficient:

The Props assist the House—
Until the House is built—
And then the Props withdraw
And adequate, erect,
The House supports itself—
And cease to recollect
The Augur and the Carpenter—
Just such a retrospect
Hath the perfected Life—
A past of Plank and Nail—
And slowness—then the Scaffolds drop
Affirming it a Soul.

(#1142, P,801. Version to Sue.)

Like the poems it echoes: 'This Consciousness that/is aware' and 'I'm ceded—I've stopped being Their's' (#508), this is a poem about the soul's autonomy, about the poet's 'coming of age.' For Dickinson, the 'past of Plank and Nail'—with its crucifixion imagery—was indeed a painful one but it was also the fire in which her soul was forged. And it is this soul, a soul that lived out the divisions of being a woman and being a poet in Dickinson's society without being destroyed by them, a soul that burned with 'unannointed blaze,' a soul that was a 'theatre' for every role the human heart could play, that Dickinson celebrates her poetry. To Dickinson, this soul in all its multiform diversity was a 'Granitic /Base' (#789, F,875). Indeed, insofar as it was 'Finite Infinity,' it was God.

Chapter Five

Of Genre, Gender and Sex

[The clitoris] is endowed with the most intense erotic sensibility, and is probably the prime seat of that peculiar life power, although not the sole one.

(Charles D. Meigs, 1851)

> Forbidden Fruit a flavor has
> That lawful Orchards mocks—
> How luscious lies within the Pod
> The Pea that Duty locks—
> (Emily Dickinson, c. 1876)

Long before Harold Bloom was a gleam in his mother's eye, Charles D. Meigs, Professor of Midwifery at the University of Pennsylvania, delivered himself of the opinion that no woman could be a strong poet. In a chapter on 'Sexual Peculiarities' (qualities distinguishing the sexes) in *Woman: Her Diseases and Remedies*, his 1851 textbook on gynecology, Meigs declared,

150

Of Genre, Gender and Sex

She composes no Iliad, no Aeneid. The strength of Milton's poetic vision was far beyond her fine and delicate perceptions. She would have been affrighted at the idea of that fiery sea on whose flaming billows Satan,

> 'With head uplift above the waves, and eyes
> That sparkling blazed_____
>   extended long and large,
> Lay floating many a rood: in bulk as huge
> As whom the fables name of monstrous size;
>   _____or that sea-beast
> Leviathan, which God of all his works
> Created hugest that swim the ocean stream.'

'Do you think,' Meigs continues in full sentimentalist rapture, 'that a woman, who can produce a race and modify the whole fabric of society, could have developed in the tender soil of her intellect, the strong idea of a Hamlet, or a Macbeth? . . . Such is not woman's province, nature, power, nor mission.'[1]

There is no way of knowing whether Meigs was aware of the phallic symbolism in the lines he quoted. It is possible that Milton himself was not conscious of it. But the doctor's belief in women's literary impotence, her 'castration,' could hardly have been better served. To Meigs, biology determined woman's poetic as well as her reproductive and moral destiny. She neither should, not could, write like a man. Meigs was not alone in this conviction. The young Austin Dickinson (age 22) appears to have held a similar belief—at least so his sister Emily thought. Reprimanded by her brother for writing in too 'exalted' a style, Dickinson retorted:

> you say you dont comprehend me, you want a simpler style. *Gratitude* indeed for all my fine philosophy! I strove to be exalted thinking I might reach *you* and while I pant and struggle and climb the nearest cloud, you walk out very

leisurely in your slippers from Empyrean, and without the *slightest* notice request me to get down! As *simple* as you please, the *simplest* sort of simple—I'll be a little ninny—a little pussy catty, a little Red Riding Hood, I'll wear a Bee in my Bonnet, and a Rose bud in my hair.

(L,117)

No giant leviathans for her, extending their bulk, long and large, as they float lengthwise on burning lakes. If she wants to be a good girl (a girl who knows her place), she will be a 'little ninny,' a 'little pussy catty,' a rosebud or a bee. And the 'simplicity' of her writing, its intellectual and stylistic 'littleness,' will match her adorably miniature size. A woman who tried to reach higher, as the poet says she did in her letter to Austin, was sure to get cut down. And the worst of it was her male adversary did not even have to put on his shoes in order to demolish her. His place was in the 'Empyrean.' Hers was on the ground.

Since Dickinson labored long and hard over her letters, her hurt and outrage at Austin's criticism are understandable. Her brother had cut her where it mattered most: in her potential as a writer. And whether or not Austin actually saw style in gender terms (since his letters to his sister were destroyed, we have only her word), Dickinson obviously believed that he did. Like strong ideas, high style was a masculine preserve (a male cloud, a gendered 'Empyrean'), and men intended to keep it that way, no matter how talented or even gifted a particular woman writer might be.

By 1862, the presumed date of 'I think I was enchanted' (#593), dedicated to her chosen precursor, Elizabeth Barrett Browning, Emily Dickinson seems to have accepted the idea—if she ever toyed with it seriously—that she should not try to write like a man.

Even more than Barrett Browning, who put her hand to political verse and the domesticated epic, notably in *Aurora Leigh*—indeed, even more than poets like Sigourney and Oakes-Smith, who also wrote in forms other than the personal lyric—Dickinson was prepared to stay within strict genre expectations for women's poetry. Neither her style—nor her particular set of abilities—lent themselves to the length and breadth of epic structures, to high style or strong writing in a masculine sense.

'I had no Monarch in my life, and cannot rule myself, and when I try to organize—my little Force explodes—and leaves me bare and charred,' she told Higginson in August of that year (L,414). While the submerged parallel to orgasm may have been fortuitous, it was not out of place. Dickinson was no Homer or Milton, or even Wordsworth of the philosophical poems, to spread her bulk out upon the page. She lacked the organizing skills and the grand view of herself as writer, necessary for epic length and voice. From her point of view, she also may have lacked the organ. But neither was Emily Dickinson a ninny.

How could a woman write 'like a woman' and still be 'strong'? For men, the concept of potency carries with it an inevitable *double entendre*, which, as we know, male authors have made the most of over time. From Homer and Milton to Whitman and Mailer, the concepts of creative power and sexual power have been intertwined in the masculinist literary tradition. Male writers have felt free to glorify their sex, to identify, as Gilbert and Gubar observe, their penises with their pens.[2]

But the 'hidden' nature of female sexuality has, historically, made the identification between sexual power and personal power much more difficult for women than it is for men. Indeed, as Sigourney's 'Alpine Flowers' makes clear, such an identification requires a tolerance

153

for paradox that few people, male or female, would find easy to sustain, especially when confronted with critics like Austin Dickinson and Charles Meigs.[3] For a writer of personal lyrics, like Dickinson, to believe that she could be 'strong' required a 'Conversion of the Mind' equivalent, as she says in the poem on Barrett Browning, to seeing bees as butterflies and butterflies as swans. For it meant that somehow the 'little' could also be 'great,' that the rosebud could be a source of power—that, to switch to another favored Dickinson metaphor for hidden (not just repressed but underestimated) female power, volcanoes could grow 'at Home' (#1705, P,1153).[4] It meant, in short, that the impossible could be.

This chapter will discuss patterns of genital imagery in Dickinson's work which suggest that she experienced female sexuality (and female creativity) as a separate and autonomous power equal to, but different from, men's own: a 'little' but 'explosive' force. Since this discussion will be based on the analysis of image patterns whose sexual significance may have been hidden from the poet on a conscious level, it is bound to seem speculative. Without external evidence, there is no way to know how deliberate Dickinson's use of this imagery was. But sexual symbolism, particularly genital symbolism, derives from the deepest levels of the psyche and frequently lies outside conscious control. What matters is not Dickinson's conscious awareness of the sexual significance of this imagery, but the role these images play contextually in her work and the kinds of meanings that accrue intertextually around them.

A network of specifically female genital images, including both the vagina and the clitoris (represented in Dickinson's poetry by persistent references to crumbs, berries, peas, pearls and other small, round objects), pervades her work. Taken together, these images suggest that both Dickinson's sexuality *and* her imagination were homoerotic and autoerotic, that is, they were preferentially centered on female sexuality, whether or not the poet was actively sexual with women. Interpreted with an eye to biography, these images also suggest that this female-centered eroticism was one of the primary enabling factors in Dickinson's emergence as a strong woman poet.

As a nineteenth-century woman, Emily Dickinson was sexually and poetically disempowered by the society in which she lived. Even in his slippers, her brother Austin could kick her off his cloud. He, not she, was entitled to 'exalted' style and 'strong ideas.' But in the letters and poems discussed in this chapter, Dickinson implies that she found another kind of power in being a woman (in having vaginal as well as oral lips, in possessing a 'crumb' if not a 'loaf'). However small or hidden this power was— like the volcano's crater or like the rosebud (indeed, like the clitoris itself)—in its own way it was great.

Dickinson's female sexual imagery makes its first appearance, not surprisingly, in her youthful letters to women friends. Like most middle-class women in her culture, Dickinson's early romantic attachments were with members of her own sex. And her letters to two women in particular—Susan Gilbert, her future sister-in-law, and Kate Scott Anthon, a widowed friend of Susan's—are permeated with erotic suggestiveness. In these letters Dickinson invests the commonplace identification of women with flowers with an oral emphasis that will characterize her use of female sexual imagery throughout her life. To Gilbert, she writes in 1852:

Only think of it, Susie; I had'nt any appetite, nor any Lover, either, so I made the best of fate, and gathered antique stones, and your little flowers of moss opened their lips and spoke to me, so I was not alone.

(L,202)

and in 1853:

It *is sweet* to talk, dear Susie, with those whom God has given us, lest we should be alone—and you and I have *tasted it*, and found it *very sweet*; even as fragrant flowers, o'er which the bee hums and lingers, and hums *more* for the lingering.

(L,221)

In 1859, she sent Anthon, with whom she had a brief but exceedingly passionate romantic friendship, the following challenge-invitation:[5]

Dare you dwell in the *East* where we dwell? Are you afraid of the Sun?—When you hear the new violet sucking her way among the sods, shall you be *resolute*? . . .

. . . And should new flower smile at limited associates, pray her remember, were there *many* they were not worn upon the breast—but tilled in the pasture! So I rise, wearing her—so I sleep, holding,—Sleep at last with her fast in my hand and wake bearing my flower.

(L,349–50)

Women in these passages are flowers. As flowers, they (or their sexual parts) are to be held, savored, lingered over and physically enjoyed. Indeed, Dickinson suggests that, properly 'tasted,' the sweetness she and her friends share can substitute for other missing physical and emotional goods: food and male lovers. While their love may appear 'little' (after all, their 'antique stones' and 'flowers of moss' are small), Dickinson is prepared to make 'the best of fate' since her fear of the 'Sun' (the heat of male love) is much greater than any regret she might experience respecting the 'small' dimensions of a woman-to-woman affection.

From the often-quoted 'man of noon' letter, we know that Dickinson did, in fact, view romantic friendships between women as both 'smaller' than and preferable to the love of men.[6] In this letter, written to Gilbert a year prior to the latter's engagement to Austin in 1853, Dickinson depicts male sexuality in no uncertain terms as a force destructive to women. It is a 'sun' that 'scorches' and 'scathes' them and Dickinson is eager to warn Susan, whom she loved exorbitantly, away from it:

> you have seen flowers at morning, *satisfied* with the dew, and those same sweet flowers at noon with their heads bowed in anguish before the mighty sun. . . . Oh, Susie, it is dangerous, and it is all too dear, these simple trusting spirits, and the spirits mightier, which we cannot resist!
>
> (L,210)

As in the letter to Anthon, written seven years later, what Dickinson hoped was that Gilbert would be '*satisfied* with the dew' (the 'East'), that is, with women. Unfortunately, perhaps, for Austin as much as for the poet, she did not get her wish.

From the first of three draft letters commonly believed to have been written to one individual, the so-called 'Master,' it appears that Dickinson herself fell in love with a man not long after writing the letter to Anthon cited above. But if she did, her need for close affective ties with women did not substantially change. On the contrary, Dickinson's commitment to romantic friendship (especially her love for Susan) not only survived the period when her passion for the Master presumably reached its peak (1860–2) but lasted long after it came to an end—by 1865, when he ceases to figure significantly in her poetry. Whatever its status in actuality (whether real or a product of the poet's imagination), Dickinson's relationship with this man was not the shaping experience of her life. Not was it, as it is sometimes made out to be, the formative influence on her art.[7]

As Adalaide Morris and Margaret Homans have separately argued, Dickinson represents her (or her speaker's) relationship with the Master in terms of hierarchy, difference and domination.[8] (I would add, violence.) On the woman's part, it was a relationship of perfervid emotional activity in which the speaker is frequently in danger of losing herself. In her letters and poems, Dickinson employs the conventional terms of male power and female powerlessness which she uses in the 'man of noon' letter, with, unhappily, predictable results. Overwhelmed by her lover's masculine 'superiority,' the speaker becomes the pathetic flower-wife Dickinson claimed in her letter to Susan she dreaded to be:

> Oh, did I offend it—[Did'nt it want me to tell it the truth] Daisy—Daisy—offend it—who bends her smaller life to his (it's) meeker (lower) every day—who only asks—a task— [who] something to do for love of it—some little way she cannot guess to make that master glad
>
> (L,391)

So closely does Dickinson identify the male lover with the male governing principle that in some poems it is impossible to tell whom the speaker is addressing: a lover or God. 'A Wife—at Daybreak I shall be' (#461) and 'He found my Being—set it up' (#603) are examples.[9]

In such poems and the many like them, Dickinson's

lovers take on their socially-constructed roles. What is even more distressing, the poet takes on woman's traditional linguistic subordination as well. Poem #246 opens on a biblical/Miltonic note:

Forever at His side to walk—
The smaller of the two!
Brain of His Brain—
Blood of His Blood—
Two lives—One being—now
(from #246, F,215)

The beginning of #275 is just as predictable if more Barrett-Browningesque:[10]

Doubt Me! My Dĭm Companion!
Why, God, would be content
With but a fraction of the Lĭfe—
Poured thee, without a stint—
The whole of me—forever—
What more the Woman can,
Say quick, thăt I may
dower thee
With lăst Delight I own!

+faint Companion—
+of the love—
+so I can—
+least Delight—
(from #275, F,249)

The conventionality of these latter poems—so strikingly at odds with Dickinson's most characteristic work—is significant. When imagining her speaker in love with a man, Dickinson was apparently unable to conceive of relationship (or a language in which to express it) that did not conform to heterosexuality's cultural inscription. Women were smaller, weaker and less empowered than

159

men; men *vis-à-vis* women were gods. Women owed them all. While the depiction of this state of dependency could result in poems of great and even tender passion, as in 'He touched me, so I live to know' (#506), it was passion rooted in the acceptance of female lack. As such, it could lead just as easily to moments of intense self-abnegation and the panicky rejection of personal power, as in 'If He *dissolve*—then—there is *nothing—more*' (#236).

In her recent defense of Dickinson's heterosexual love poetry, '"Oh Vision of Language"',' Margaret Homans argues that Dickinson resolves the power issues raised by her heterosexual poetry in her love-after-death poems. Since poems like 'If I may have it when it's dead' (#577) start from a position of original difference, Homans asserts, they are able to 'open up new kinds of linguistic meaning' in a way that Dickinson's homoerotic poetry—which depends on 'sameness'—cannot.[11] But even if this were true (which I question), the hierarchical conception of love upon which the love-after-death poems depend for their original meaning did nothing for the poet here. In Heaven, Dickinson's lovers may be equal; but on earth they are not. On earth, the speaker—emotionally as well as linguistically identified with her subordination—accepts the helplessness of her situation entirely. In such poems, the result is not 'new meaning,' but some of the most disturbing and at the same time archetypically 'feminine' poetry that Dickinson wrote:

Why make it doubt—it
hurts it so—
So sick—to guess—
So strong—to know—
So brave—upon it's little
Bed

To tell the very last They
said
Unto Itself—and smile—
And shake—
For that dear—distant—
dangerous—Sake—
But—the Instead—
the Pinching fear
That Something—it did
do—or dare—
Offend the Vision—and
it flee—
And They no more remember me—
Nor ever turn to tell me Why—
Oh, Master, This is Misery—

(#462, F,782)

The speaker of this poem is not in control. Not only is the poem painful to read but it smacks of the most degrading kind of female self-abasement. If, as Ann Case asserts, 'what the lover genuinely and universally loves is the act of imagination itself,' then when it comes to heterosexuality, Dickinson's love for her 'act of imagination' was as dangerous to her as she feared it would be, and she was right to want to protect herself against it.[12]

Precisely because her love for the Master could elicit such contradictory and risky self-representations, Dickinson's heterosexual love poetry is absorbing to read. For good or ill, this poetry bares all, illuminating, as Helen McNeil says, 'the steps by which this dark path [i.e., self-punitive masochism] is prepared for the "different".'[13] As such, it demonstrates all too effectively how Western sexual arrangements and the discourse in which they are embodied have helped mold women psychologically to embrace and identify with weakness, lack and pain.

But, for all the intensity and passion she brought to it,

161

heterosexuality was not a source of poetic or psycho-logical strength for the poet. At best, it was a means of assuming (or stealing, as in 'The Daisy follows soft the Sun' [#106]) another's power so that the woman becomes 'Brain of his Brain,' wore *his* crown.[14] At worst, it was a savage reminder of how weak she was. Like the struggle over high style, the struggle for sexual equality was not a battle Dickinson could win—at least not on the terms her culture provided. More important, perhaps, *it could not be won on the terms her imagination had absorbed.* Whatever men might be in heaven, in life, and, more particularly, in her own mind, they were 'mightier.' Although she might fantasize standing equal to them, there is no evidence in her writing that she actually thought she could.

It is specifically in contrast to this kind of hierarchically-arranged (and ultimately destructive) relationship that Emily Dickinson presents romantic friendships with women in her poetry. As both Homans and Morris observe, Dickinson's woman-centered poetry is based on sameness rather than difference. As a result, it lacks the potential for the kind of fervor and angst characteriz-ing her poetry to the Master—both the drama of the speaker's 'elevation' (her 'Queenship') and the pathos and anguish of her 'fall.' Instead, it is, for the most part, like her nature poetry. That is, it is a poetry of 'little' things: birds, bees, flowers, dew, crusts and crumbs, images which Dickinson employs to represent a love that, from her point of view, is correspondingly 'small.'

Of her relationship with Samuel Bowles's wife, Mary, she declares, *c.* 1859:

Her breast is fit for pearls,
But I was not a "Diver"—
Her brow is fit for thrones
But I have not a crest.
Her heart is fit for *home*—
I—a Sparrow—build there
Sweet of twigs and twine
My perennial nest.
(#84, P,68–9. Version to Samuel Bowles.)

And to Susan she wrote *c.* 1860:

A little bread, a crust—a crumb,
A little trust, a Demijohn!
Can keep the soul alive,
Not portly—mind!
But breathing—warm—
Conscious, as old Napoleon,
The night before the Crown!

A modest lot, a fame petite,
A brief Campaign of sting and sweet,
Is plenty; is enough!
A sailor's business is *the Shore*,
A *soldier's—Balls*!
Who asketh more
Must seek the neighboring life!
(#159, P,116. Version to Sue.)

The emphasis on smallness, mutuality and nurturance in
these poems hardly needs stressing. Dickinson's speaker
is not a king with a 'crest,' or a soldier with '*Balls*'
(about as direct as the poet ever gets regarding male sex-
ual anatomy).[15] Lacking the ultimate signifier of sexual
difference, she cannot furnish her beloved with the
riches that come from loving a man, from loving, that is,

someone who has more 'wealth' (identified with the phallus) than herself.

But if the love between women is a 'modest lot,' it is also a 'lot' in a second sense. That is, it occurs in and is identified with the poet's backyard—with the flowers and bees, the bread women bake, the demijohns of home-made wine they enjoy together. (Like many nineteenth-century women, Dickinson and her friends not only baked their own bread but raised their own grapes and made their own wine.) These items compose the 'neighboring life,' shared—as so much was shared—between Dickinson and other women, not just Susan but Mrs Bowles, Mrs Holland, the Norcross cousins and her sister Vinnie. It was a life—and love—of equality and mutual nurturance: of twigs and twine and, of course, of 'sting and sweet.' 'You love me—you are sure,' Dickinson asks Sue (whom she identifies in this poem as '"Dollie"'):

> I'll bear it better now—
> If you'll just tell me so—
> Than when—a little dull
> Balm grown—
> Over this pain of mine—
> You sting—again!
> (from #156, F,158–9)

In a brief poem sketched on a scrap of paper *c.* 1881, the poet sums up a lifetime of mutual loving and fighting, presumably with Susan:

> 'Tis Seasons since the Dimpled War
> In which we each were Conqueror
> And each of us were slain
> And Centuries 'twill be and more
> Another Massacre before

So modest and so vain—
Without a Formula we fought
Each was to each the Pink Redoubt—
(#1529, P,1054)

Whatever differences they had, the tie between them, as
Dickinson told Susan in late 1885, never dissolved
(L,893). Its very mutuality—the mutuality of their joined
lives as well as of their sameness—was the basis of its
strength.

Equally important in ''Tis Seasons since the Dimpled
War,' however, is the poet's claim—whether or not
entirely justified—that the relationship she is describing
represents a new kind of discourse as well as a different
kind of love. It is a 'Dimpled War' (a love match as well as
a match between lovers) fought '[w]ithout a Formula,'
outside conventions and in a new way. Freed from the
hierarchical framework imposed by 'compulsory hetero-
sexuality,' as Adrienne Rich calls it, the two women
become 'Each . . . to each [a] pink Redoubt.' That is, they
become a defended *and* a secure place to each other (a
sort of fortified *hortus conclusus* or barricaded garden of
love). And to judge by the awkwardness of some of the
language in this poem, Dickinson was struggling to find
a new way to represent this love, one that would capture
its novelty as well as its oxymoronic power (its modesty
and vanity) without reference to the male or to the
phallus woman lacks, that is, without reference to
Difference with a capital 'D.'[16]

It is within the context of these poems on romantic
friendship that Dickinson's specifically erotic poetry
must be read. Although Dickinson wrote sexual poems
that seem clearly directed toward the Master, her most
important and characteristic erotic poetry is all written
from within this same concept of 'sameness.' That is, it is

written in a homoerotic mode, whether or not it is explicitly homoerotic. Profoundly attracted to the female body, Dickinson lets her love for it inform her erotic poetry even when she is, or seems to be, writing heterosexual verse. Not only does she focus on female sexual power, but the 'lover' who is invited to share this power is rarely specified as a human male. Most often, he is a male bee and, hence, being small and round, ambiguously a covert female symbol. A few examples will illustrate what I mean:

> Come slowly—Eden!
> Lips unused to Thee—
> Bashful—sip thy Jessamines—
> As the fainting Bee—
>
> Reaching late his flower,
> Round her chamber hums—
> Counts his nectars—
> Enters—and is lost in Balms.
> > (#211, F,190)

> Did the Harebell loose her girdle
> To the lover Bee
> Would the Bee the Harebell *hallow*
> Much as formerly?
>
> Did the "Paradise"—persuaded—
> Yield her moat of pearl—
> Would the Eden *be* an Eden
> Or the Earl— an *Earl*?
> > (#213, P,149)

> Rowing in Eden—
> Ah! the Sea!
> Might I but moor—
> Tonight—
> In Thee!
> > (from #249, F,222)

166

Reading these poems as they blend into one another through repeated patterns of imagery, one can hardly help noticing that they are all written from an ambiguous point of view.[17] They are about the joys of entering but who is doing the entering? Where does the speaker stand? With whom does she identify? Not only are the poems imbricated with layer upon layer of female sexual imagery—Eden, lips, bashful, sip, jessamine, faint, flower, round, chamber, nectar, balm, girdle, Paradise, yield, pearl, sea—but Dickinson focuses entirely on the delight these images project. The speaker's awareness of the sheer physical enjoyment of female sexuality, symbolized by the idea of losing oneself in balms, is almost overwhelming. Despite minor differences, all the poems say the same thing: a woman's vagina is a wonderful place in which to be lost. It is that paradisical land of milk and honey where, presumably, we would all like to go.

That Dickinson fantasized entering this paradise (and tasting this honey) seems evident from some of her less ambiguously homoerotic poems. She sent her cousin Eudocia (Converse) Flynt, for example, the following poem with a flower, most likely a rose:

All the letters I could write,
Were not fair as this—
Syllables of Velvet—
Sentences of Plush—
Depths of Ruby, undrained—
Hid, Lip, for Thee,
Play it were a Humming Bird
And sipped just Me—
(#334, P,268. Version to Eudocia Flynt.)[18]

Since Dickinson sent this poem to a cousin, she may well have considered it innocent. But it is not an innocent poem. Read exclusively at the level of its sexual imagery—

the undrained ruby 'Depths,' the emphasis on playing and sipping, etc.—it is an invitation to cunnilingus—the form of erotic activity to which, consciously or unconsciously, Dickinson appears to have been most drawn. By the penultimate lines, poem, flower and speaker are identified with each other and the hidden depths of the poet-speaker's ruby vagina-mouth are offered up for her cousin (reader) to sip, 'lip' to lips. Given that Dickinson chose to write this invitation from the point of view of one who can speak knowingly of the delights she describes, her sexual orientation in it seems clear. The pleasures she is representing are ones she presumably has savored (or, more probably, fantasized savoring) herself. Otherwise, she would not offer them with such enthusiasm—and authority—to her (female) reader.

But if the more obviously homoerotic poems suggest that Dickinson fantasized sexual relations with women, they also suggest that she may have confined her desires to fantasy life. Romantic friendships were encouraged between nineteenth-century middle-class women. Sexual relations, particularly those involving penetration, were not. In writing of her homoerotic desires, Dickinson typically solved the problem posed by this cultural taboo by leaving the reality of the experience she describes in doubt. Thus in poem #518, she undercuts the affirmation of her opening lines by questioning whether or not the experience they describe is a dream:

> Her sweet Weight on my
> Heart a Night
> Had scarcely deigned to lie—
> When, stirring, for Belief's
> Delight,
> My bride had slipped
> away—

If 'twas a Dream—made
solid—just
The Heaven to confirm—
Or if Myself were dreamed of Her—
The +power to presume—

With Him remain—who unto Me—
Gave—even as to All—
A Fiction superseding Faith—
By so much—as 'twas real—

+wisdom

(#518, F,671)[19]

While in #1722, she shifts the burden of disbelief to the
reader, giving the sceptical a way out:

Her face was in a bed of hair,
Like flowers in a plot—
Her hand was whiter than the sperm
That feeds the sacred light.
Her tongue more tender than the tune
That totters in the leaves—
Who hears may be incredulous,
Who witnesses, believes.

4. sacred] central   5. tune] tone
5. tender] timid/magic

(#1722, P,1161)

Both these poems deny and assert at once. Both partake
therefore of the irreducible ambiguity of fantasy or
dream. Nevertheless, on one point they are clear.
Imagery based on erotic engagement with the female
body had become for Dickinson the symbol for a certain
kind of physical/sexual good, whether or not that good
was achievable in real life. To experience the female body
(the face in its bed of [pubic?] hair, the tongue that totters
in the leaves, the sweet weight), was to experience 'A

169

Fiction superseding Faith—/By so much—as 'twas real.'[20] As Dickinson says frequently, here and elsewhere, it was to experience the equivalent of heaven, the more so precisely because it was unrealizable in this life.

Like her fantasies of equality between male and female lovers, Dickinson's poems on the physical fulfillment of love between women were also a testimony, in Homans's words, to the poet's acceptance of 'the idea that the best experience can take place only in the realm of the imagination.'[21] And Dickinson's homoerotic poetry is, therefore, as much a search for ways to open up 'new meaning' (to make possible through imaginative rescripting what otherwise could not be) as is her poetry on love-after-death, indeed far more necessarily so.

In a striking and perhaps fortuitous parallel to Sappho, first noted by the lesbian poet Judy Grahn,[22] Dickinson compares the paradise of the female beloved to the highest apple on the tree:

"Heaven"—is what I cannot
reach!
The Apple on the Tree—
Provided it do hopeless—hang—
That—"Heaven" is—to Me!

The Color, on the Cruising Cloud—
The interdicted Land—
Behind the Hill—the House
behind—
There—Paradise—is found!

Her teazing Purples—Afternoons—
The credulous—decoy—
Enamored—of the Conjurer—
That spurned us—Yesterday!
(#239, F,292)

To Sappho, it was the untouched maiden who hung like an apple on the topmost branch of the tree 'not once noticed by/harvesters or if/not unnoticed, not reached.'[23] To Dickinson, it appears to have been the woman next door—as noted earlier, Susan's house lay *west* of the Homestead—who teased the poet with her evening 'Purples,' the color of the sunset, royalty and love. Susan was 'the House/behind' the hill (the mons Veneris?), that never could be entered, the forbidden land for which the poet longed, the illusion she loved though it 'spurned [her]—Yesterday!' Above all, Susan was simply woman, possessed in the poet's own body and in her fantasy life, and unpossessable, at once.

There are only two poems in the Dickinson canon in which her speaker appears to fantasize actively engaging in sexual relations with a man: 'He was weak, and I was strong—then' (#190) and 'I rose—because He sank' (#616). As their title lines suggest, both poems are framed as contests for power and both are chillingly fleshless exercises as a result. For warmth, for honey and for balm, it was to fantasies of female sexuality that Dickinson turned. And it was within this basically homoerotic (and autoerotic) context that she came to define her own desire. In the poetry privileging the clitoris, Dickinson puts into words her subjective awareness of this desire, and its paradoxical little-big nature.

In *Literary Women*, Ellen Moers notes that women writers—including Dickinson—have a predilection for metaphors of smallness which Moers relates to their small physical size. 'Littleness,' she writes, 'is inescapably associated with the female body, and as long as writers describe women they will all make use of the diminutive in language and the miniature in imagery.' Even though Moers summarizes these metaphors suggestively as 'the little hard nut, the living stone, something precious in miniature to be fondled with the hand or cast away in wrath,' she does not identify such images as clitoral.[24] However, if we are to understand how a great many women—not just Dickinson, but Sigourney and others—have traditionally chosen to represent their 'difference' to themselves, such an identification seems necessary.

As early nineteenth-century gynecologists like Meigs were aware (a knowledge suppressed later in the century), the clitoris is the 'prime seat' of erotic sensibility in woman just as its homologue, the penis, is the prime seat in man.[25] It is reasonable to assume, therefore, that the clitoris's size, shape and function contribute as much to a woman's sense of self—her inner perception of her power—as do those of her vagina or womb—the sexual organs which psychoanalytic critics since Freud have chosen to privilege.[26] Images of 'smallness' in women's writing unquestionably relate to woman's body size and to her social position—even as we saw in Sigourney's poem. But like phallic images (which also serve these other purposes), such images have a sexual base, and so does the power women so paradoxically attribute to them. In identifying their 'little hard nut[s]'—or their little flowers—with 'something precious,' women are expressing through the paradoxes of their symbolism their body's subjective consciousness of itself. That is, they are expressing their conscious or unconscious awareness of the organic foundation of their (oxymoronic) sexual power.[27]

The existence of a pattern of imagery involving small, round objects in Dickinson's writing cannot be disputed.[28] Whether identified as male or female, bees alone appear 125 times in her poetry. Dews, crumbs, pearls and berries occur 111 times, and with peas, pebbles, pellets, beads and nuts, the total number of such images comes to 261. In the context of the poems in which they appear, many of these images seem neutral, that is, they appear to have no sexual significance. But their repetitiveness is another matter. So is the way in which they are given primacy in many poems. Analysis of the latter suggests that on the deepest psychological level, these images represented to the poet her subjective awareness of her female sexual self: both its 'littleness' when compared externally to male sex (the internal dimensions of the clitoris are another matter) and the tremendous force nevertheless contained within it. In privileging this imagery, consciously or unconsciously, Dickinson was replacing the hierarchies of phallocentric discourse—hierarchies that disempowered her as a woman and as a poet—with a (paradoxical) clitorocentrism of her own. Insofar as it established that something might be 'little' and *great* at the same time, this clitorocentrism affirmed her specifically female sexual and creative power.

Over and over clitoral images appear in Dickinson's poetry as symbols of an indeterminate good in which she delights yet which she views as contradictory in one way or another. It is small yet great, modest yet vain, not enough yet all she needs. The following poem brings together many of these motifs:

God gave a Loaf to every Bird—
But just a Crumb—to Me—
I dare not eat it—tho'
I starve—
My poignant luxury—

To own it—touch it—
Prove the feat—that made
the Pellet mine—
Too happy—+for my Sparrow's chance—
For Ampler Coveting—
                    +in
It might be Famine—all around—
I could not miss an Ear—
Such Plenty smiles upon my Board—
My Garner shows so fair—

I wonder how the Rich—may feel—
An Indiaman—An Earl—
I deem that I—with but a Crumb—
Am Sovreign of them all—

                                        (#791, F,884)

There are a number of things to note here. First, the
poet is undecided whether the crumb in her possession
satisfies her physical or her material appetite. In the first
three stanzas it takes care of her hunger (albeit, by
touching). In the fourth stanza it makes her wealthy, an
'Indiaman' or 'Earl.' She also cannot decide whether or
not she is starving. For while she can touch and feel the
crumb, she cannot eat it. Owning it, therefore, is a con-
tradictory business. It is a 'poignant luxury,' that is, a
deeply affecting, possibly hurtful, sumptuousness that
has overtones of archaic *lust*. Finally, poor though she
is, the crumb makes this sparrow a 'Sovreign,' that is, it
gives her power. She prefers it to 'an Ear,' presumably an
ear of corn, and hence, given the poem's erotic suggest-
iveness, a phallus.

From one point of view, this poem is, obviously, a
stunning example of Dickinson's use of indeterminate
imagery. Despite the many terms whose status as erotic
signifiers can be established by reference to passages

elsewhere in her work (loaf, bird, eat, luxury, sparrow, famine, plenty, Indiaman, earl, sovereign), there is no way to 'know,' finally, what the poem is about.[29] Not only do masturbation and cunnilingus fit but so do having a male or female lover, having some other unnamed good instead, sharing communion with God and being content with her small/great lot as poet.

But even if this is true, what matters is that Dickinson has used imagery based upon her body as the primary vehicle through which to make her point. Whether or not she actually intended this poem to be 'about' the clitoris, the clitoris is the one physical item in a woman's possession that pulls together the poem's disparate and conflicting parts. What other *single* crumb satisfies a woman's appetite even though she cannot eat it, and gives her the power of a 'Sovreign' (potent male) whoever she is? In trying to represent her sense of self and the paradoxes of her female situation, consciously or unconsciously, Dickinson was drawn to what she loved most: the body she inhabited, the body she loved in other women as well as in herself. And it is the specific and extraordinary power of this body, its 'Sovreign' littleness, that she celebrates in this poem.

'God gave a Loaf to every Bird' puts the multiple ambiguities of a poem like 'I had been hungry, all the/ Years,' discussed in the previous chapter, in a new light. Despite the latter poem's similar indeterminacy, it, too, represents the speaker grappling with the paradoxes of her appetite. Identifying with birds, who by nature and in nature ('Nature's—Dining Room'), share a 'Crumb,' the speaker in this poem also contrasts her lean diet with the 'Loaf' that others—presumably men and married women—possess. By the time the poem is over, however, she too reverses her stand. Entering the room where the 'ample/Bread' lies (also identified with 'the/Wealth/I

175

could not hope—for Mine'), she discovers that 'Plenty hurt[s]':

> 'twas so
> new—
> Myself felt ill—and odd—
> As Berry—of a Mountain Bush—
> Transplanted—to the Road—
>
> Nor was I hungry—so I
> found
> That Hunger—was a way
> Of Persons outside Windows—
> The Entering—takes away—
> (#579, F,331–2)

Recognizing the *difference* in her appetite not only changes the speaker's notion of self (the transplanted 'Berry'), it also changes the value she places on what others desire. Put bluntly, heterosexuality—the only way women can possess the 'Wealth' of the phallus/loaf—loses its mystery and appeal when experienced close up.

In contrast to 'God gave a Loaf,' 'I had been hungry, all the/Years' ends on an ironic, inconclusive note, which can be read as either self-affirmation (the good you possess is an illusion) or denial (since I cannot handle it, I do not want it). But on the level of its sexual imagery, the poem's main point is clear. Whether or not it was a matter of choice, Dickinson believed that her appetite/desire distinguished her from others. She was not at home in the houses where others lived nor did she travel the roads they walked. 'Crumbs' were all she was suited for.

In other poems, Dickinson writes playfully and joyfully of the qualities which set her appetite/desire (and therefore her self—her 'Berry') apart:

As the Starved Maelstrom
laps the Navies
As the Vulture teazed
Forces the Broods in
lonely Valleys
As the Tiger eased

By but a Crumb of
Blood, fasts Scarlet
Till he meet a Man
Dainty adorned with
Veins and Tissues
And partakes—his Tongue

Cooled by the Morsel
for a Moment
Grows a fiercer thing
Till he esteem his Dates
and Cocoa
A Nutrition mean

I, of a finer Famine
Deem my Supper dry
For but a Berry of
Domingo
And a Torrid Eye—
                    (#872, F,1102–3)

Unlike 'God gave a Loaf' and 'I had been hungry, all the/ Years,' which signify on a variety of different levels, 'As the Starved Maelstrom' is a poem which, the critical literature suggests, makes little sense without reference to the clitoral imagery privileged within it.[30] In the first three stanzas, the speaker compares male appetite sequentially—and hyperbolically—to a whirlpool, a vulture and a man-eating tiger. In the final stanza, she celebrates her own 'finer Famine,' satisfied with 'a Berry of/Domingo/And a Torrid Eye.' The 'male-storm'[31] of blood and lust which the speaker depicts in the first three stanzas of this poem is so blatantly exaggerated it seems meant to be humorous. Men, the speaker claims, are so voracious they will devour anything, including, finally, themselves. (I read both 'Crumb of Blood' and 'Dates and Cocoa' as allusions to women.) In the final stanza, the speaker proudly asserts her own 'limited' appetite by way of comparison. It is this appetite which defines her, making her what she is: 'I, of a finer famine.'

Whether Dickinson satisfied her appetite in reality, or, as is more probable, only in autoerotic fantasy (masturbation), does not matter. 'Emblem,' she wrote to Higginson in 1883, 'is immeasurable—that is why it is better than Fulfillment, which can be drained' (L,773). For Dickinson, the limitless gratification of 'Emblem' (that is, of symbolic representation), satisfied her to the end of her life. In 1864, the same year in which she wrote 'As the Starved Maelstrom/laps the Navies,' she sent Susan the following letter/poem. I give the text as it appears in holograph, not as Johnson presents it in the variorum edition:

The luxury to
apprehend
The luxury 'twould
be
To look at Thee
a single time
An Epicure of Me
In whatsoever
Presence makes
Till for a further
food
I scarcely recollect
to starve
So first am I

supplied—
The luxury to
meditate
The luxury it was
To banquet on
thy Countenance
A Sumptuousness
bestows
On plainer Days,
Whose Table, far
As Certainty—can see—
Is laden with a
single Crumb—
The Consciousness—
of Thee.
                    Emily.
(#815, H341. Version to Sue.)[32]

And in a letter written to Susan *c.* 1883, she declared: 'To be Susan is Imagination,/To have been Susan, a Dream—/What depths of Domingo in that torrid Spirit!' (L,791). Over the twenty years that intervened between the poems and this letter, Dickinson's patterns of female sexual imagery and the homoerotic values that these patterns encoded did not substantially change. Taken together, they were the 'emblems' that satisfied her in a way that reality, for whatever reason, could not. They were the highest 'Apple on the Tree.'

As in so many things, Dickinson viewed her sexuality with compound vision in a highly complex, paradoxical light (as small and great, impoverished and sumptuous, vulnerable and powerful). Where her figurative patterns suggest that she saw male sexuality (like other forms of power which she gendered masculine from God to death) as destructive to women—it scorched them and destroyed their will, it was a plenty that hurt, a vulture that lapped up navies, a Tiger uneased by crumbs of blood, a frost that killed—female sexuality had the power to feed and nourish her even when she thought herself deprived. Insofar as it contained both elements (sumptuousness and destitution), this concept of female sexuality validated the poet's view of herself and of her poetry: unknown yet great, a 'Child' yet still a 'Queen,' a rosebud that could speak with power.

It is my belief that Dickinson's ability to transcend the limitations placed upon her gender and to pose female sexuality and female creativity as valid, autonomous *alternatives* to male sexuality and male creativity is directly rooted in her homoerotic and autoerotic commitment to women. In particular, this ability reflects her willingness to see in women and in her own woman's body sources of love, power and pleasure ('luxury') independent of what Mary Lyon calls 'the other sex.'[33] Like her nature poetry, her use of female sexual imagery suggests, therefore, not the 'subversion' of an existing male tradition nor the 'theft' of male power—but rather the assertion of a concept of female sexuality and female creativity that renders male sexuality and the poetic discourse around male sexuality irrelevant.

To Dickinson each woman had the potential to be her own 'Pink Redoubt.' In her own body and in the bodies of other women she could discover all the love, pleasure and power she needed. Like the 'little force' that produced Dickinson's highly explosive poems, her female sexuality was 'little' but it was 'enough.'

Conclusion

What the French call *jouissance*, Dickinson called bliss (or transport or ecstasy) and she experienced it with astonishing regularity in a wide variety of contexts: reading Elizabeth Barrett Browning, writing poetry that left her 'bare and charred,' watching a robin take flight, contemplating sunset, or dawn, looking at stalks of witchhazel, loving her own body. It was an experience for which she lacked precise words:

As if I asked a common Alms,
And in my wondering hand
A Stranger pressed a Kingdom,
And I, bewildered, stand—
As if I asked the Orient
Had it for me a Morn,
And it should lift it's purple Dikes,
And shatter me with Dawn!
(#323, P,253. Version to T. W. Higginson.)

And, as this poem suggests, it was an experience for

which she sought words over and over again. For it was this experience—explosive, transformative, bewitching, erotic, wondrous, shattering—from which Dickinson produced her poetry. It marked her as the agent of her own desire and the creator of her own discourse, allowing her to reach an orgasm that was an act of poetry and an act of love together. Like that other orgasm, it blinded, lightened and consumed at once:

> To pile like Thunder to it's close
> Then crumble grand away
> While Everything created hid
> This—would be Poetry—
>
> Or Love—the two coeval come—
> We both and neither prove—
> Experience either and consume—
> For None see God and live—
>
> (#1247, P,866)

It let her 'see God' and live.

In *This Sex Which Is Not One*, Luce Irigaray observes that women in Western society are fundamentally alienated from their sexuality by their object status within the dominant phallic economy. Instead of being agents of their own desire or creating their own discourse, they masquerade. 'In the last analysis,' she writes, 'the female Oedipus complex is woman's entry into a system of values that is not hers, and in which she can "appear" and circulate only when enveloped in the needs/desires/fantasies of others, namely, men.'[1] For women to escape this masquerade, Irigaray argues, they must dig beneath the layers of heterosexuality to a sexuality that is auto-erotic and homoerotic at once. Like the twin lips of the vulva this sexuality will take pleasure touching itself.[2] For Irigaray, the expression of this sexuality will require a new syntax, for in it there would 'no longer be either subject or object' and '"oneness" would no longer be privileged.'[3] At the conclusion of *This Sex Which Is Not One*, Irigaray provides an extended homoerotic pan-egyric, modelling the linguistic innovations which she believes will characterize this new female discourse.

More than a hundred years before Irigaray, Dickinson was able to take the hesitant explorations made by her fellow women poets into nature and into their own female power and create from them a unique and fundamentally paradoxical discourse that put into words her own subjectivity as a woman and the specifics of her situation and desire. Insofar as she was able to do so, it was, I believe, because she was in touch with her homoeroticism and autoeroticism. Loving the same, she privileged sameness rather than difference. And because she did, Dickinson was able to find both in herself and in other women sources of pleasure and power independent of the other sex. Unlike so many women poets, she did not want/ expect/need man to bind *her* flower to *his* breast. As a result, she was not 'enveloped in [his] needs/desires/ [and] fantasies.' However much it may have tempted her at times, in the end she rejected the 'masquerade,' just as she rejected the 'wisdom of the ages and the nature of man.'

What also seems clear, however, is that for Dickinson, the clitoris, not the vulva (Irigaray's focus), was the primary organic foundation for the sense of autonomous sexual and creative power her poetry inscribes. While Dickinson uses many tropes for the vaginal area, including (most importantly) the volcanic one, it was the issue of 'littleness' that served as the hook for her imagination. For it was on this issue that, given her situation as a nineteenth-century woman, so much seemed to depend, and it was the potential power of this 'littleness' that she needed to prove—its 'explosive force.'

And this clitorocentrism may well explain, therefore, certain fundamental and yet anomalous features in Dickinson's work, in particular, her consistent paradoxicality, her insistence on autonomy and her emphasis on 'little/bigness' in image, form and word as well as theme. Unlike many strong women writers, Dickinson did not despise or, as Moers puts it, 'cast away in wrath,' her femininity (her 'smallness'). She accepted the 'littleness' of womanhood just as she accepted the limitations of a private domestic life—or the limitations of the small, homely stanza in which she wrote, the stanza of ballads and common songs, as well as of Watts's hymns. For she knew that, properly utilized, these limitations were freedom and this littleness was great. And it was this knowledge that allowed her to be the radically independent poet she was. Moving outside the hierarchies of phallocentric culture, hierarchies that suppressed and confined her in every way, Dickinson used her 'little force' to claim a power, agency, and desire—a *jouissance*—of her own.

Notes

Introduction

1. See Cheryl Walker, *The Nightingale's Burden: Women Poets
   and American Culture before 1900* (Bloomington: Indiana
   University Press, 1982), pp. 87–95 and *passim*. Other
   helpful discussions of nineteenth-century women writers
   include Elizabeth K. Helsinger, Robin Lauterbach Sheets
   and William Veeder, *The Woman Question: Society and
   Literature in Britain and America, 1837–1883*, 3 vols (Chicago
   and London: University of Chicago Press, 1989), III; Mary
   Kelley, *Private Woman, Public Stage: Literary Domesticity in
   Nineteenth-Century America* (New York and Oxford: Oxford
   University Press, 1984); David S. Reynolds, *Beneath the
   American Renaissance: The Subversive Imagination in the Age of
   Emerson and Melville* (New York: Alfred A. Knopf, 1988),
   pp. 337–437; and Emily Stipes Watts, *The Poetry of American
   Women from 1632–1943* (Austin and London: University of
   Texas Press, 1977), pp. 83–147.

   Joanne Dobson's *Dickinson and the Strategies of Reticence:
   The Woman Writer in Nineteenth-Century America* (Blooming-
   ton and Indianapolis: Indiana University Press, 1989) came
   out too late to be assimilated into this text. However, like

myself, Dobson is concerned with placing Dickinson in respect to other American women writers of her period.

2. Caroline May, *The American Female Poets: With Biographical and Critical Notices* (Philadelphia: Lindsay & Blakiston, 1848), p. 181. Subsequent references to this anthology will be cited parenthetically in the text as 'May' followed by the page number. While not as fulsome—or intellectually demanding—as Griswold's anthology, May's volume gives a better feel for how the average woman poet of this period was seen by her female audience, and, perhaps, by herself. Griswold's volume appears to be primarily directed toward a male audience.

3. Evelyn Banning, *Helen Hunt Jackson* (New York: Vanguard Press, 1973), pp. 99–100. Also see Walker, *Nightingale's Burden*, pp. 91–9.

4. See Reynolds, *Beneath the American Renaissance*, pp. 395–412 for a discussion of what he calls 'the literature of misery' writers, after a soubriquet applied by Samuel Bowles. These are prose writers whose anger and scepticism respecting female roles spills over explicitly into their writing. By the last quarter of the century, dark thoughts begin to appear in the work of women poets as well. Cf. Rose Terry Cooke's 'Saint Symphorien,' in which a mother complains to God of her son's martyrdom, 'The flesh rebels. I am his mother./Thou didst not give me any other./Thine only Son?—but I am human./Art thou not God?—I am a woman,' and Elaine Goodale's 'Indian Pipe,' which begins: 'Death in the wood,—/Death, and the scent of decay;/Death and a horror that creeps with the blood,/And stiffens the limbs to clay,' in *Scribner's Monthly* (December, 1879), XIX, 198. The two poems appear in a special section devoted to women poets.

5. Ann Douglas, *The Feminization of American Culture* (New York: Anchor Press, 1988), pp. 17–79. For more balanced, but less extensive, treatments of women's share in this phenomenon see Gail Parker, *The Oven Birds: American Women on Womanhood, 1820–1920* (Garden City: Doubleday & Co., 1972), pp. 1–69; and Carroll Smith-Rosenberg, *Disorderly Conduct: Visions of Gender in Victorian America* (New York: Alfred A. Knopf, 1985), pp. 129–64 and *passim*, and 'Writing History: Language, Class, and Gender,' in

Feminist Studies/Critical Studies, edited by Teresa de Lauretis (Bloomington: Indiana University Press, 1986), pp. 31–54. Also helpful are Colleen McDanell, *The Christian Home in Victorian America, 1840–1900* (Bloomington: Indiana University Press, 1986); and Mary P. Ryan, *The Empire of the Mother: American Writing about Domesticity, 1830–1860* (New York and London: Harrington Park Press, 1985).

6. Walker, *Nightingale's Burden*, p. 86.
7. Smith-Rosenberg, 'Writing History' in de Lauretis, *Feminist Studies/Critical Studies*, p. 40.
8. Reynolds, *Beneath the American Renaissance*, pp. 387–90. In *The Woman Question*, Helsinger, Sheets and Veeder discuss the various ways in which the doctrine of true womanhood (and the entire question of woman's nature) was open to debate by the second half of the nineteenth century. However, even where activity outside the home was justified, the grounds for this justification still rested on women's superior moral nature (what the three authors call the concept of the 'Angel out of the House') and, equally important, women were still expected to devote themselves to the ideals of usefulness and service (II, xv, 109–64).
9. *The Mother's Journal and Family Visitant* (Philadelphia, 1851), XVI, 16.
10. *The Power of Christian Benevolence Illustrated in the Life and Labors of Mary Lyon*, edited by Edward Hitchcock (Northampton, Mass.: Hopkins, Bridgman, & Company, 1852), p. 191.
11. *Mother's Journal*, XVII, 119.
12. Emily Norcross Dickinson was the least articulate member of this highly verbal family, and her situation has remained something of an enigma. However it seems evident that she was depressed for much of her married life. See Richard B. Sewall in *The Life of Emily Dickinson*, 2 vols (New York: Farrar, Straus & Giroux, 1974), I, 74–90; John Cody in *After Great Pain: The Inner Life of Emily Dickinson* (Cambridge, Mass.: The Belknap Press of Harvard University Press, 1971), pp. 39–103 and *passim*; and Cynthia Griffin Wolff in *Emily Dickinson* (New York: Alfred A. Knopf, 1986), pp. 36–65 and *passim*. The recent publication of Emily Norcross's courtship letters to Edward Dickinson make it clear that from the beginning, her husband overwhelmed her

verbally, as in most other respects. See *A Poet's Parents: The Courtship Letters of Emily Norcross and Edward Dickinson*, edited by Vivian R. Pollak (Chapel Hill and London: University of North Carolina Press, 1988). Pollak's final judgment that 'hers was not a strongly articulated personality, and she never achieved a clearly defined identity, except as a dependent' probably represents the best we can do (p. 217).

13. Jane Tompkins, *Sensational Designs: The Cultural Work of American Fiction, 1790–1860* (New York and Oxford: Oxford University Press, 1985), pp. 127–46. The difference between Stowe and Dickinson is the difference between a writer who looks out toward family and society in order to effect change and one whose concerns are largely psychological and metaphysical. In this sense Dickinson refused the most obvious form of power sentimentalism had to offer.

14. Feminist critics have treated this theme from a variety of different perspectives. See in particular Wendy Martin, *An American Triptych: Anne Bradstreet, Emily Dickinson, Adrienne Rich* (Chapel Hill and London: University of North Carolina Press, 1984), pp. 148–64; Barbara Antonina Clarke Mossberg, *Emily Dickinson: When a Writer is a Daughter* (Bloomington: Indiana University Press, 1982), pp. 99–112 and *passim*; and Elizabeth Phillips, *Emily Dickinson: Personae and Performance* (University Park and London: Pennsylvania State University Press, 1988), pp. 6–26.

15. Walker, *Nightingale's Burden*, p. 88.

16. As quoted in Richard B. Sewall, *The Lyman Letters: New Light on Emily Dickinson and Her Family* (Amherst, Mass.: University of Massachusetts Press, 1965), p. 69. Martha Bianchi's portrait of her Aunt is most fully drawn in *Emily Dickinson: Face to Face* (Cambridge, Mass.: Houghton Mifflin Company, 1932). Her vision of Dickinson as a white moth is corroborated by Jackson in an 1876 letter to the poet reprinted in *The Letters of Emily Dickinson*, edited by Thomas H. Johnson and Theodora Ward, 3 vols (Cambridge, Mass.: The Belknap Press of Harvard University Press, 1958), II, 565. Subsequent references to this edition of Dickinson's letters will be cited parenthetically in the text as 'L,' followed by the page number. Higginson's impressions can

be gathered from his preface to the first edition of Dickinson's poetry and from his essay 'An Open Portfolio,' both reprinted in *The Recognition of Emily Dickinson*, edited by Caesar R. Blake and Carlton F. Wells (Ann Arbor, Michigan: The University of Michigan Press, 1968), pp. 3–12; and from his comments to his wife, reprinted in *The Letters of Emily Dickinson* (L,473–6 and 518–19).

17. As quoted by Sewall in *Life*, II, 377. A fuller portrait of Dickinson by Ford may be found in *Letters of Emily Dickinson*, edited by Mabel Loomis Todd, new and enlarged edition (New York and London: Harper, 1931), pp. 127–30.

18. Martha Nell Smith '"To Fill a Gap",' *San José Studies* (Fall, 1987), pp. 12–13.

19. *The Manuscript Books of Emily Dickinson*, edited by R. W. Franklin, 2 vols (Cambridge, Mass. and London: The Belknap Press of Harvard University Press, 1981), II, 1004. Subsequent citations to this edition of the poems will appear parenthetically in the text as the letter 'F,' followed by the page number. For ease of reference, the Johnson number of the poem will also be included. See also Chapter 1, n. 3 for Johnson citations.

20. Jane Donahue Eberwein, *Dickinson: The Strategies of Limitation* (Amherst: University of Massachusetts Press, 1985), p. 29.

21. As quoted in *Emily Dickinson's Home: Letters of Edward Dickinson and His Family*, edited by Millicent Todd Bingham (New York: Harper & Brothers, 1955), p. 414. I have treated Dickinson's attitude toward both housework and service to others at much greater length in *My Life A Loaded Gun: Female Creativity and Feminist Poetics* (Boston: Beacon Press, 1986), pp. 15–28.

22. Sandra Gilbert, 'The Wayward Nun Beneath the Hill: Emily Dickinson and the Mysteries of Womanhood' in *Feminist Critics Read Emily Dickinson*, edited by Suzanne Juhasz (Bloomington: Indiana University Press, 1983), p. 24.

23. Dickinson's romantic friendships have been studied by, among others, myself in *My Life A Loaded Gun*, pp. 28–55; Lillian Faderman, 'Emily Dickinson's Letters to Sue Gilbert,' *Massachusetts Review* XVIII (Summer 1977), pp. 197–225; and Adalaide Morris, '"The Love of Thee—a Prism

Be'': Men and Women in the Love Poetry of Emily Dickinson' in Juhasz, *Feminist Critics*, pp. 98–113.

24. Walker, *Nightingale's Burden*, pp. 35–6.
25. Lydia Huntley Sigourney, *Letters of Life* (New York: D. Appleton and Company, 1867), p. 376.
26. Walker, *Nightingale's Burden*, p. 34.
27. See Wendy Barker, *Lunacy of Light: Emily Dickinson and the Experience of Metaphor* (Carbondale and Edwardsville: Southern Illinois University Press, 1987), pp. 99–101, for a somewhat different interpretation of the dark/light imagery in this poem.
28. For a restrained and persuasive discussion of Dickinson's eye trouble see Phillips, *Personae and Performance*, pp. 61–75. Phillips suggests iritis (inflammation of the iris), a severe but curable condition.
29. Adrienne Rich, *On Lies, Secrets and Silence: Selected Prose 1966–1978* (New York: W. W. Norton, 1979), pp. 158–63.
30. The problematics of de-centering the subject in women's writing are discussed in essays by Nancy K. Miller and Tania Modleski in de Lauretis, *Feminist Studies/Critical Studies* and in essays by Elaine Showalter, Nina Baym, and Jane Marcus in *Feminist Issues in Literary Scholarship*, edited by Shari Benstock (Bloomington and Indianapolis: Indiana University Press, 1987).

Chapter One

1. Douglas, *Feminization of American Culture*, pp. 3–13.
2. *The Complete Works of Ralph Waldo Emerson*, (Boston and New York: The Riverside Press, 1904), IX, 37–8.
3. *The Poems of Emily Dickinson*, edited by Thomas H. Johnson, 3 vols (Cambridge, Mass.: The Belknap Press of Harvard University Press, 1958), III, 1048 (poem #1519). Subsequent citations from this edition will appear parenthetically in the text as the letter 'P,' followed by the page number on which the poem appears. Variants will be placed at the bottom and identified by line number.
4. This play on the color yellow was apparently part of the Dickinson family verbal repertoire. See Martha Dickinson's postscript to a letter to her brother, Ned, 'Why do we

fear the preacher at the first church is threatened with
Jaundice? Because he is such a *yell'er!'* As quoted by Barton
Levi St. Armand ' "Your Prodigal": Letters from Ned Dick-
inson, 1879–1885,' *The New England Quarterly*, LXI (Sep-
tember, 1988), pp. 367–8.

5. Cristanne Miller, *Emily Dickinson: A Poet's Grammar*
(Cambridge, Mass. and London: Harvard University
Press, 1987), p. 46. I am extending Miller's grammatical
conception of disjunction to include logical categories.

6. Miller, *A Poet's Grammar*, pp. 37–9.

7. Miller, *A Poet's Grammar*, p. 46.

8. Andrew Lang, 'Some American Poets,' in Blake and
Wells, *Recognition*, p. 37.

9. David Porter, *Dickinson: The Modern Idiom* (Cambridge,
Mass. and London: Harvard University Press, 1981), p. 7.

10. Higginson, 'Preface,' in Blake and Wells, *Recognition*, p. 12.
Cf. Reviews by Arlo Bates, and William Dean Howells in
the same volume.

11. Referencing Emerson, Joanne Feit Diehl locates Dickin-
son's notion of the abyss in the ungraspability of nature.
I locate it in the ungraspability of transcendent meaning.
The implications of this difference for our reading of Dick-
inson's nature poetry will become apparent in Chapter 3.
See *Dickinson and the Romantic Imagination* (Princeton:
Princeton University Press, 1981), pp. 170–82. And see
Chapter 4, n. 3.

12. Miller, *A Poet's Grammar*, p. 46. Recent criticism has
located this poem, which is central to John Cody's argu-
ment for Dickinson's psychotic breakdown, in the poet's
response to the death of Frazer Stearns in 1862 in the Battle
of Newborn. That Dickinson was responding to the death
of a young man in war seems more probable than that she
was writing retrospectively about a nervous breakdown.
However, in either case, what is most important about the
poem is the epistemological, ontological and teleological
conclusions which the poet drew from the 'event'—what-
ever it was. See Cody, *After Great Pain*, pp. 291–355; Barton
Levi St. Armand, *Emily Dickinson and Her Culture: The
Soul's Society* (New York and Cambridge: Cambridge
University Press, 1984), pp. 104–9; and Phillips, *Personae
and Performance*, pp. 46–50.

13. See Wolff for a discussion of Dickinson's use of the 'plank' as an emblematic image, e.g., the 'plank' of faith, *Dickinson*, pp. 229–30. Dickinson's use of this common image is doubtless over-determined.

14. Porter, *The Modern Idiom*, p. 7.

15. See Porter, *The Modern Idiom*, pp. 81–142 and *passim*. Porter's brilliant phenomenological analysis of Dickinson's poetic is, unfortunately, undermined by his determination to link the poet with what he views as destructive trends in modernism. As a result, he cannot validate her commitment to process even though he describes it eloquently. E.g.,

> Each of her attempts was an original birth. In among the variants, we trace the moment when figures crucial to individual poems are created from phenomenological experience. They are high-risk performances in defiance of the drag of familiar language patterns. In this engagement we come close to the hidden precinct where, as Ernst Gombrich has said of the creative act, the angel stands guard with the flaming sword (p. 36).

16. See Susan Howe, 'Some Notes on Visual Intentionality In Emily Dickinson,' *HOW(ever)*, vol. III, no. 4, pp. 11–13 and 'Women and Their Effect in the Distance,' *Ironwood* #28, vol. XIV, no. 2, pp. 78–9. Although Porter was the first to call attention to the way in which formal publication has distorted our impression of Dickinson's poetry, it is Howe who has forced the issue, by insisting that Dickinson's lineation, margins, spacing, and the various other 'accidentals' of her texts are necessary clues to her poetic practice and to her sense of self as poet. In normalizing them, Howe argues, Johnson has ignored the poet's 'radical rejection of Poetry as a commodity,'

> *He* [Johnson] called his Introduction 'Creating the Poems' then gave their creator a male muse-Minister. *He* arranged her 'verses' into hymn-like stanzas with little variation in form and no variation in cadence. By choosing a sovereign system for her line endings—*his* preappointed Plan, he established the constraints of a strained positivity. Copious footnotes, numbers, comparisons, and chronologies mask his authorial status.
> ('Some Notes,' *HOW(ever)*, p. 11)

What is lost, Howe declares, is our sense of 'the open processual character' of Dickinson's writing ('Women and Their Effect,' *Ironwood*, p. 79).

Whether or not all the 'accidentals,' which Howe insists must be maintained in their integrity, were deliberate on Dickinson's part, Howe's principal thesis is one with which even Porter would have to agree. The only edition of Dickinson's poetry which will accurately represent what she wrote *the way she wrote it* will be one that duplicates all the idiosyncracies of her manuscripts. How or whether this can be managed in a printed text, I do not know. But I would note here that Howe's determination to stick with the manuscripts permits her (like Porter in his own way) to give the most sensitive reading of Dickinson's poetic I have encountered. To evade the manuscript problem is to evade Dickinson. Indeed, it is to read another poet, the poet created, as Porter admonishes, by print.

17. Sandra M. Gilbert and Susan Gubar, *The Madwoman in the Attic: The Woman Writer and the Nineteenth-Century Literary Imagination* (New Haven and London: Yale University Press, 1979), pp. 634–5.

18. Miller, *A Poet's Grammar*, p. 49.

19. Dickinson's discontinuance of the fascicles and some of the other anomalies of her later manuscripts are frequently attributed to worsening eye trouble; but extremely severe eye trouble did not prevent a writer like James Joyce from seeing his manuscripts into print. Had Dickinson *valued* the concept of 'fair copy' (a fixed version), she would have found some way to achieve it. By the late 1870s it is clear she no longer did—if she ever really had.

Chapter Two

1. Cynthia Griffin Wolff has made the most thorough-going effort to rationalize Dickinson's spiritual development, with mixed success. See *Dickinson*, pp. 139–59, 260–365, and 523–37, in particular.

2. Reynolds, *Beneath the American Renaissance*, p. 37.

3. Although virtually every Dickinson critic recognizes that the poet rebelled against the Calvinist concept of deity (her

protest can hardly be missed), only St. Armand suggests that nineteenth-century sentimentalism may have contributed to her disaffection. However, he confines his discussion to the impact that secular concepts of a 'religion of love' had upon her (*Dickinson and Her Culture*, pp. 120–51). Karl Keller provides a sensitive and persuasive treatment of the complexities of Dickinson's ambivalence toward Puritanism in *The Only Kangeroo Among The Beauty: Emily Dickinson and America* (Baltimore and London: Johns Hopkins University Press, 1979), pp. 38–124. My discussion will be limited to the single strand of the poet's resistance to the concept of a sovereign God.

4. Douglas, *The Feminization of American Culture*, pp. 32–43. See also Richard Forrer, *Theodicies in Conflict: A Dilemma in Puritan Ethics and Nineteenth-Century American Literature* (New York: Greenwood Press, 1986), pp. 1–98. Forrer provides a much more balanced view of the theological and political issues involved in the demise of Puritanism than does Douglas, who focuses mainly on what she sees as the debilitating effects of female sentimentalism. I am very much indebted to his discussion.

5. As quoted by Forrer, *Theodicies in Conflict*, p. 45.

6. Jonathan Edwards, *The Works of Jonathan Edwards*, revised and corrected by Edward Hickman, 2 vols (Edinburgh and Pennsylvania: The Banner of Truth Trust, 1979), II, 7.

7. Edwards, *Works*, II, 528.

8. Forrer, *Theodicies in Conflict*, p. 64.

9. Douglas, *Feminization of American Culture*, p. 24.

10. As quoted by Forrer, *Theodicies in Conflict*, p. 84.

11. William E. Channing, *The Works of William E. Channing* (Boston: American Unitarian Association, 1875), p. 467.

12. Channing, *Works*, p. 296.

13. Douglas, *Feminization of American Culture*, p. 137.

14. See Parker, *Oven Birds*, p. 13: 'Sentimentalism restructured the Calvinist mode of salvation, making the capacity to feel, and above all to weep, in itself evidence of redemption.'

15. See Douglas, *Feminization of American Culture*, pp. 200–26, for an extended discussion of these qualities.

16. *Hymns for Mothers and Children* (Boston: Walker Fuller & Company, 1866), p. 150. There is no way of knowing who

marked this poem but the place-mark itself, 'Tessie's Trial,' by Ella Ricker, is one that would have delighted Dickinson. The poem, clipped from a newspaper, represents the complaint of a young woman whose mother makes her stay inside on a beautiful spring day so that she can sew a quilt: 'I know she loves me dearly,/But oh, she cannot dream/How hard it is in spring-time/To sit and sew a seam!' Since Dickinson seems to have had a habit of leaving odd place-marks in books, e.g. flowers, bits of cloth, string, ribbons, etc., it is possible that she left the poem there. If so, then it may be an oblique comment on Taylor's platitudinous assumption that God cares how children feel.

17. Douglas, *Feminization of American Culture*, p. 122.
18. St. Armand, *Emily Dickinson*, p. 123.
19. Wolff, *Dickinson*, pp. 142–7 and *passim*. Taking Dickinson's identification with Jacob as central to her poetic and psychological development, Wolff organizes her entire biography around it. While I also see this identification as central to Dickinson's *religious* poetry, I am not prepared to extend it globally to Dickinson's work in other genres. Like Shakespeare, Dickinson made her values genre-dependent and, as we shall see in the next chapter, the world of her nature poetry is a very different place from that depicted in her religious verse.
20. Wolff, *Dickinson*, pp. 118–36.
21. In a poem such as this, Dickinson seems to be removing the onus of original sin—if not of sinfulness—from mankind. Not only does she question the historicity of Moses, but the poem blames God for not seeing his servant accurately (as innocent). As she says in another poem 'Whether Deity's guiltless—/My business is to find!' (#178, F,146). This question, not her own sinfulness, or even mankind's, is the one that consumes her.
22. In *The Romantic Imagination*, Diehl argues that this poem could not be about God since God would not conduct 'public rituals of worship, singing songs in praise of Divinity' (p. 156). But it is precisely in these narcissistic terms that God was envisioned by Puritans on both sides of the Atlantic. See Douglas, *Feminization of American Culture*, p. 122.

23. Douglas, *Feminization of American Culture*, p. 200.
24. Wolff, *Dickinson*, p. 50.
25. Traditional criticism of Dickinson has attributed her concern with death either to her personal pathology or to her metaphysical dilemma. But recent attempts to situate the poet in her cultural context have considerably broadened our understanding of Dickinson's 'obsession.' Besides the Wolff biography, see Shira Wolosky, *Emily Dickinson: A Voice of War* (New Haven and London: Yale University Press, 1984) for a full-length study of the impact that the Civil War had upon the poet. Also see St. Armand, *Dickinson and her Culture*, pp. 104–15; and Phillips, *Personae and Performance*, pp. 46–60.
26. Wolff, *Dickinson*, p. 344. 'There is,' Wolff notes 'appalling whimsy in the image of God-the-amateur-empiricist— puttering in His workshop, trying now this and now that new creation.' I would add that in so far as God relates to the beings he creates/destroys in the same way that the scientist/inventor relates to nature (that is, appropriatively), this poem tacitly genders mankind as female. (See Chapter 3, n. 12, below.)
27. Dickinson, *Poems*, III, 1070. As Dickinson herself makes clear, the conclusions she states here are far more likely to represent her response to *fin de siècle* doubt than to the death of a loved one.
28. Keller, *Only Kangeroo*, pp. 67–8, 94–6.
29. It is possible that this silence is the result of denial (if I am damned, I do not want to think about it). But it is also possible that Dickinson decided she was a likely candidate for salvation. Certainly, she was not shy about speculating on what it would be like in heaven after she died.

Chapter Three

1. In a note accompanying this poem, Dickinson wrote '"Sanctuary Privileges" for Ned, as he is unable to attend' (L,732). The phrase "Sanctuary Privileges" was apparently family code for not attending church. See St. Armand, 'Letters from Ned Dickinson,' *NEQ*, pp. 367–9.
2. Wolff, *Dickinson*, pp. 94–104.

Notes

3. *Mother's Journal*, XVI, 97.
4. Gilbert, '"Wayward Nun",' in Juhasz, *Feminist Critics*, p. 41.
5. Dickinson refers to the Madonna in two poems, #s 648 and 918, and in seven letters, #s 675, 820, 886, 903, 925, 977, 979 (as 'the "Holy Family"'). The Madonna underwent a revival in Protestant circles as a figure for Christian motherhood during the nineteenth century. See McDannel, *The Christian Home*, p. 130, and Helsinger, Sheets and Veeder, *The Woman Question*, II, 194–9. To my knowledge, Dickinson's association of the Madonna with mother nature is unique.
6. Wendy Martin, *An American Triptych*, pp. 83 and 155. Martin is the first critic to present Dickinson's relationship to nature within the context of her domestic relationships with women. I am much indebted to her study.
7. In one text, women are instructed in such matters as paper flowers, feather work, hair work, bouquets of oak leaves and crosses of flowers. See Mrs C. S. Jones and Henry T. Williams, *Ladies Fancy Work: Hints and Helps to Home Taste and Recreations* (New York: Henry T. Williams, 1876). Also see E. A. Maling, *A Handbook for Ladies on In-Door Plants, Flowers for Ornament, and Song Birds* (London: Smith, Elder & Co., 1867) and Shirley Hibbard, *Rustic Adornments for Home and Taste and Recreations for Town Folk in the Study and Imitation of Nature* (London: Groombridge & Sons, 1856), for British examples of the genre. Hibbard was male, but his book is addressed to women.
8. Elizabeth Barrett Browning, *The Poems of Elizabeth Barrett Browning* (New York: James Miller, 1867), IV, 14–15.
9. Louis Agassiz, 'Methods of Study in Natural History,' *The Atlantic Monthly*, IX (January, 1862), p. 5.
10. Emerson, *Works*, I, 66. Actually, in this passage Emerson critiques scientific inquiry into nature of the type in which Agassiz engages, preferring 'untaught sallies of the spirit' instead. But both men represent theoretical approaches typical of the masculinist (Platonic) tradition. See n. 12 below.
11. Emerson, *Works*, I, 19.
12. Margaret Homans, *Women Writers and Poetic Identity: Dorothy Wordsworth, Emily Brontë, and Emily Dickinson*

(Princeton: Princeton University Press, 1980), pp. 18 and
190–1. Homans argues, however, that Emerson's disinterest
in a concept of 'Mother Nature' helped prevent Dickinson
from identifying too closely with a concept of female
nature—an identification which, Homans believes, would
have silenced her. This is a position with which I emphatic-
ally disagree. Not only does the subtext of *Nature* gender
material nature as female (and hence untrustworthy), but
it is, as I hope to show, precisely from this nature (*natura
naturata*) that Dickinson's most vivid and forceful figures
come. Emerson's ambivalence respecting the female has
been brilliantly deconstructed by David Leverenz in his
essay, 'The Politics of Emerson's Man-Making Words,' in
Speaking of Gender, edited by Elaine Showalter (New York
and London: Routledge, 1989), pp. 134–62.

The differences between the way men and women
relate to nature has been one of the most fruitful areas of
feminist inquiry since the inception of the second wave.
See, most recently, Evelyn Fox Keller's thoughtful series
of essays on the relationship between gender and science,
Reflections on Gender and Science (New Haven and London:
Yale University Press, 1985). 'Naming nature is the special
business of science,' she begins, with an allusion to
Emerson's well-known essay:

> What classically distinguishes knowledge is its essential thrust
> away from the body: its ambition is to transcend the carnal.
> Mind is not simply immanent in matter; it is transcendent over
> it. All visions of knowledge must accordingly struggle with the
> dialectic between immanence and transcendence. What is
> especially striking is how often the metaphoric field for this
> struggle is that of sex and gender, and . . . how deeply those
> metaphors have influenced the discipline of knowledge (pp.
> 17 and 18).

I would submit that much of the tension in Dickinson's
poetry derives from her 'female' identification with mater-
ial nature in a culture that, intellectually-speaking, was
largely committed to a Platonic/Emersonian concept of
Mind. Put another way, I believe that if 'the metaphoric
field for this struggle is that of sex and gender,' then
Dickinson's relationship to nature (and her nature poetry)
can rightly be called homoerotic.

13. *Leaf and Flower Pictures, and How to Make Them* (New York: Anson D. F. Randolph, 1857), p. 9.

14. Besides Hale, at least three other women put together flower/poetry books around this period: Mrs Elizabeth Wirt, *Flora's Dictionary* (Baltimore: F. Lucas, 1829); Mrs Catherine Esling, *Flora's Lexicon: An Interpretation of the Language and Sentiments of Flowers* (Philadelphia: Hooker & Claxton, 1839); and Frances Osgood, *The Poetry of Flowers and Flowers of Poetry, to which are added a simple treatise on botany, with familiar examples, and a copious floral Dictionary* (New York: J. C. Riker, 1841). 'Calendars' of birds are less common but see H. E. Parkhurst, *The Birds' Calendar* (New York: Charles Scribner's Sons, 1894). It is worth noting that—like Dickinson's nature poetry—these books show a fruitful mingling of natural science with aesthetic appreciation and sentimental fancies. Dickinson was by no means unique among women poets in putting her extensive education in the natural sciences to work in behalf of her art; most middle-class women in her day were trained as amateur naturalists and those who engaged in artistic pursuits utilized their knowledge. Sewall discusses Dickinson's education in science and its impact on her poetry in his biography, *Life*, II, 342–57.

15. Henrietta Dumont, *The Floral Offering: A Token of Affection and Esteem; Comprising The Language and Poetry of Flowers* (Philadelphia: H. C. Beck & Theo. Bliss, 1851); Mrs C. M. Badger, *Wild Flowers Drawn and Colored from Nature*, with an introduction by Mrs L. H. Sigourney (New York: Charles Scribner, 1859); L. Clarkson, *Indian Summer: Autumn Poems and Sketches* (New York: E. P. Dutton & Co., 1883). The first text in this tradition to pick up poetry by Dickinson for inclusion is Mrs William Starr Dana's field guide to flowers. See *According To Season. Talks About Flowers In The Order Of Their Appearance In the Woods and Fields* (New York: Charles Scribner's Sons, 1894), pp. 50 and 130. The copy in the author's possession is of particular interest since it has nine original watercolors by a woman artist, scattered through the text.

16. I have somewhat modified a line from a 'sentiment' by James N. Barker, included in *Flora's Interpreter*. The original reads, 'She sketched from nature well, and

studied flowers/Which was enough alone to love her for.'
Mrs Sarah J. Hale, *Flora Interpreter: Or, The American Book of
Flowers and Sentiments*, fourteenth edition, improved
(Boston: Thomas H. Webb & Co., 1837), p. 127.

17. Hale, *Flora's Interpreter*, p. 247. See, Annie Finch, 'The Sentimental Poetess in the World: Metaphor and Subjectivity in Lydia Sigourney's Nature Poetry,' *Legacy* V (Fall, 1988), pp. 3–18, for a different but stimulating approach to Sigourney's nature poetry.

18. St. Armand, *Dickinson and Her Culture*, p. 237. See pp. 219–97 for his discussion of the pictorial roots of Dickinson's nature poetry in the work of male aestheticians such as Asher B. Durand of the Hudson River School and John Ruskin. At the very least, Dickinson was—as St. Armand says—'domesticating' their theories, i.e. she was bringing them within the chosen purview of women's art.

19. Dickinson, of course, also depicted thunderstorms whose effects were ultimately more violent, as in 'The Wind begun to knead the Grass,' in which a tree is quartered (#824). But what is most striking about her treatment of storms is her consistent use of domestic imagery, cutting the storm down, as it were, to size. Thus in 'The Wind begun to knead the Grass,' the poem opens with a female figure (kneading) and closes with a happy escape (the house is not damaged). In 'The Lightning is a yellow Fork,' the sky is a large table and lightning bolts are 'awful Cutlery' (#1173, P,819). In 'A Cap of Lead across the Sky/ Was tight and surly drawn,' the opening figure makes the storm sound more like a balky schoolboy than a force of nature (#1649, P,1128). Since Dickinson sent a number of these storm poems to women friends (Susan, Mrs Holland), she was probably having fun with them: not bringing dread into the known—as some critics have argued—but bringing the known into dread. See Diehl, *The Romantic Imagination*, pp. 128–9, and St. Armand, *Dickinson and Her Culture*, pp. 244–9, for an opposite point of view.

20. For a discussion of the exotic qualities of the imagery in this poem see Rebecca Patterson, *Emily Dickinson's Imagery*, edited with an introduction by Margaret H. Freeman (Amherst: University of Massachusetts Press, 1979), pp. 146–7 and 149.

21. Crawford H. Greenwalt, *Hummingbirds* (New York: Doubleday & Co., 1960), p. 9.
22. Morris, '"The Love of Thee",' in Juhasz, *Feminist Critics*, pp. 107–8.
23. Mrs Frederic Tuckerman was the happy recipient of 'The Dandelion's pallid tube,' together with a pressed dandelion.
24. Badger, *Wild Flowers*, p. 2.
25. The difference in quality between Badger's delicately rendered prints, which are faithful to their subject, and her poems, which are, unhappily, sentimentalism at its worst, is striking. Her lines on the arbutus are typical: 'When hath May's sun or April's softening shower,/ Warm'd into life a less assuming flower/Than simple me, in pale pink vesture drest/While close to earth my lowly head finds rest?' Yet Dickinson was not above using them. About 1875, she sent Sue a poem on the arbutus, which begins: 'Pink—small—and punctual—/Aromatic—low—/ Covert—in April—/Candid—in May' (#1332, P,920). She signed it 'Arbutus—.'
26. Naomi Schor, *Reading in Detail: Aesthetics and the Feminine* (New York and London: Methuen, 1987), p. 4. See also Schor's original essay on the detail as clitoral, 'Female Paranoia: The Case for Psychoanalytical Feminist Criticism,' *Yale French Studies* (1981), LXII, 204–19. As will become apparent in Chapter 5, I believe that Schor's work has important ramifications for women's writing and may speak to one of the ways in which women's art has historically distinguished itself from men's.
27. Lucy Larcom, *Landscape in American Poetry* (New York: D. Appleton and Co., 1879), p. 89.
28. Individual studies of birds and flowers appear rarely in the works of the major male poets (Longfellow, Whittier, Bryant, Emerson, Lowell), on an average of three or four times per poet. Even Lowell's 'The Nightingale in the Study,' to which Larcom refers, has Calderon as its real subject, not the catbird: 'Bird of today, thy songs are stale/ To his, my singer of all weathers,/My Calderon, my nightingale,/My Arab soul in Spanish feathers.' *The Complete Poetical Works of James Russell Lowell* (Boston and New York: The Riverside Press, 1896), p. 331.

29. The point here is that for Dickinson, 'Heaven'—'Bliss'—
was an affective experience, even (as I shall suggest in
the conclusion), an orgasmic one, precipitated by sense
experience. It did not come from the apprehension of the
presence of God in nature but from the experience of
nature-in-itself. This is what 'healed.'

I should also stress that there is no way that a poem such
as 'A Bird came down the Walk' can be accommodated to
aesthetic practices based on a concept of the sublime.
While artists and poets of the sublime (e.g. the Hudson
River School) were concerned with detail, detail had to be
subordinated to the whole. Light and dark, contrast and
continuity, were achieved through a harmonization of
parts. The whole figured forth the divine. At the very
least, however, it is impossible to make the two parts of
Dickinson's poem mesh.

For an excellent discussion of the concept of the sublime
as it entered nineteenth-century American literature see
Donald Ringe, *The Pictorial Mode: Space and Time in the Art
of Bryant, Irving & Cooper* (Lexington: University of Ken-
tucky, 1971). Also see Schor, *Reading in Detail*, pp. 11–22
for a discussion of the inherent incompatibility of focus on
detail with concepts of the sublime.

30. I am indebted to Jane Langton for identifying the 'myster-
ious apple' as a fungus gall.

31. Emerson, *Works*, III, 29.

32. Keller, *The Only Kangaroo*, p. 159.

33. Emerson, *Works*, VIII, 17.

34. St. Armand, *Dickinson and Her Culture*, pp. 231–6.

35. Indicative here is early reaction to this poem by the hostile
reviewers cited in Blake and Wells, *Recognition*, pp. 24–5 and
29. 'It is,' says one anonymous reviewer, 'clearly impossible
to scoop a tankard from pearl. The material is inadequate.'
And, of course, he is right. The kind of synesthetic trans-
ference necessary to make sense of this image can only
come when one is utterly open to sensations evoked by the
material world (the touch and feel and look of pearl, the
kinesthetic response involved in scooping, etc.).

36. Miller has analyzed the grammatical constructions in this
poem at length in *A Poet's Grammar*, pp. 2–5, 119–21 and
passim.

Notes

Chapter Four

1. In *A Poet's Grammar,* Cristanne Miller notes the similarity between 'There's a certain Slant of Light' and 'Further in Summer than the Birds,' especially in their use of the term 'Difference,' which, she comments,

   > uncannily anticipates Jacques Derrida's idea of difference and of negative or deconstructive interpretation. . . . The discourse of these poems remains on the periphery of definition. . . . Because there is no semantic or linguistic center, no focal word of origin or meaning (and in particular no Christian 'Word' that explains all), there is an expansive play of language and of analogy, which is to say of mind. (p. 102)

   These comments go to the heart of why I see these poems as dealing with 'mind' not nature. The ultimate unknowability of the relationship between *transcendent* meaning and *sense* experience is their subject, not nature *per se.*

2. I have discussed this myth at considerable length in *My Life A Loaded Gun,* pp. 72–90. See also Vivian Pollak, *The Anxiety of Gender* (Ithaca and London: Cornell University Press, 1984), pp. 83–102 and St. Armand, *Dickinson and Her Culture,* pp. 137–47 and *passim.*

3. Diehl, *The Romantic Tradition,* p. 8. Also see pp. 122–60. Diehl sees this kind of solipsism as typical of Dickinson's nature poetry and her relationship to nature. I do not.

4. Diehl, *The Romantic Tradition,* p. 49.

5. Rich, *Of Lies,* p. 167.

6. Kelley, *Private Woman,* p. 221.

7. The most extended analysis of Dickinson's psychological poetry is that by Suzanne Juhasz in *The Undiscovered Continent: Emily Dickinson and the Space of the Mind* (Bloomington: Indiana University Press, 1983). While noting the absence of all biographical information in Dickinson's poetry, Juhasz nevertheless argues for its essentially personal nature (pp. 52–4). Mossberg, Eberwein and Pollak also see Dickinson as exploring her inner self. Other feminist critics, however, have tended to see Dickinson's psychological poetry in terms of role-playing and the adoption of personae. See, for instance, Gilbert and Gubar, *The Madwoman in the Attic,* pp. 582–650; and Phillips, *Personae and Performance,* pp. 76–132. Of the

various lyric genres in which Dickinson worked, this is the poetry that has received the most searching feminist analysis.

8. Keller, *The Only Kangaroo*, pp. 56–61 and 78–81. Keller observes that in many of these poems, Dickinson does not use theological terms, but he believes her concept of self is Puritanical in origin. (See pp. 60–1.)

9. Anne Bradstreet, *The Works of Anne Bradstreet*, edited by Jeannine Hensley (Cambridge, Mass. and London: The Belknap Press of Harvard University Press, 1967), p. 247.

10. Martin, *American Triptych*, p. 53.

11. Porter's represents the most extreme and thorough-going attempt to read Dickinson as a postmodernist; but if Dickinson's language were in fact as 'autogenous' as he claims, it is unlikely that her poems would reach as many readers as they do. Wallace Stevens, Porter's avatar of 'terminal' modernism, is not a popular poet; but Dickinson, like Shakespeare, appeals to readers at every level precisely because so many of her poems manage to elude and signify at once.

12. 'Dickinson,' Juhasz writes, 'has created a "universal of the personal" that is especially characteristic of women writers' (*The Undiscovered Continent*, p. 53).

13. Jay Leyda, *The Years and Hours of Emily Dickinson*, 2 vols (New Haven: Yale University Press, 1960), I, xxi.

14. Of this and similar poems, Charles Anderson observes that Dickinson's 'best poetry is not concerned with the causes but with the qualities of pain. The qualities she sought to fix with greatest precision are its intensity, its duration, and the changes it brings about.' *Emily Dickinson's Poetry: Stairway of Surprise* (New York: Holt, Rinehart & Winston, 1960), p. 203.

15. Leyda, *Years and Hours*, I, xx.

16. Dickinson's comment to Higginson, 'When I state myself, as the Representative of the Verse—it does not mean—me—but a supposed person' (L,412), is usually taken at face value by those critics who wish to cut Dickinson's poetry off from her life. And it is certainly true that Dickinson liked to use personae, from an 'Arbutus' to 'Cole.' Indeed, the adoption of personae appears to have been a family game. (See, for example, her nephew Ned's

letter to his mother, March 29, 1883, in which he employs the voice of 'Sarah Brace,' a female gossip [St. Armand, 'Letters from Ned Dickinson,' *NEQ*, p. 363]). But Dickinson normally identifies the masks she is using. The consistency of language between her letters and her poetry (indeed, the way her poems flow out of her letters and are of one piece with them) and the fact that she was writing personal lyrics—not dramatic monologues—both argue for her poetry's biographical origins. Like Mossberg, I believe, therefore, that she was 'posing' in this comment to Higginson (*When a Writer is a Daughter*, p. 189). Her feelings, as expressed in her poetry, are 'real,' whatever caused them.

17. Archibald MacLeish, 'The Private World,' in Blake and Wells, *Recognition*, p. 307.
18. See Phillips, *Personae and Performance*, for an interpretation of Dickinson's poems as outgrowths of her reading (pp. 99–132). The problem with this method of reading is that it does not avoid the difficulty it attempts to resolve. If locating individual poems in events in Dickinson's life is simplistically 'reductive,' seeing the poems as responses to individual texts is just as reductive. Had Dickinson wanted her poems to be read in this way, like Helen Hunt Jackson, she probably would have been clear about it. Since she is not, we are left with the problem with which we began: learning how to read her poems 'her' way (i.e. without 'cause').
19. In *My Life A Loaded Gun*, I have depicted the relationship between Dickinson's psychological poetry and her biography as I understand it. I consider my argument hypothetical but hopefully plausible. Plausibility is, in my opinion, the best we can aim for.
20. Kelley, *Private Woman*, p. 221.
21. Walker, *Nightingale's Burden*, p. 27.
22. Walker, *Nightingale's Burden*, pp. 31–2. Walker feels that the presence of repressed feelings in the poetry of nineteenth-century women gives these poems autobiographical authenticity. '[A] poem like "Woman" [by Osgood] tantalizes because of its uncontrolled tensions, which suggest that the tamed autobiographical impulse is one that often sublimates a deeper need to express unconventional and

therefore unacceptable feelings' (p. 31). These latter feelings comprise, she argues, the hidden message of the text.

23. *Nightingale's Burden*, p. 47. Walker discusses this theme at length, pp. 44–8.

24. Dickinson appears to identify 'prose' with duty-bound life in a number of early letters, see letters #s 56 (to Susan Gilbert) and 65 (to Austin Dickinson) in particular. In both, 'poetry' stands for the free life of the imagination, prose for the imprisonment of 'real life.'

25. Phillips points out that Dickinson writes other poems where her persona is 'lodged in the pound,' as, for example, in 'What shall I do when the Summer troubles' (#956), where her speaker is too miserable to 'fly.' But this does not invalidate the statement of 'They shut me up in Prose,' which relates to a sense of personal freedom to *articulate*. The power to articulate would include voicing moments of despair, as well as moments of liberation. (See *Personae and Performance*, pp. 9–10.)

26. Alice Miller, *The Drama of the Gifted Child*, translated by Ruth Ward (New York: Basic Books, 1981). I am summarizing the main argument of the book.

27. Walker, *Nightingale's Burden*, p. 31. Because of the way in which the social-construct 'woman' alienates women from their own emotions, the 'false self' is a woman's issue by no means confined to the nineteenth century. See my discussion of Sylvia Plath in *My Life A Loaded Gun*, pp. 97–164.

28. Walker, *Nightingale's Burden*, p. 58.

29. Suzanne Juhasz, 'Writing Doubly: Emily Dickinson and Female Experience,' *Legacy* III (Spring 1986), pp. 5–15. Mossberg has dealt with the theme of starvation in Dickinson's poetry at length and perhaps too unilaterally. See, *When a Writer is a Daughter*, pp. 135–46. Eberwein is more appreciative of the paradoxes involved in Dickinson's treatment of her constraints, arguing that her self-imposed deprivation was one of the 'strategies' she used to intensify her poetic power. (See *Strategies of Limitation*, pp. 21–46 and 128–56.)

30. See Reynolds, *Beneath the American Renaissance*, p. 415.

Notes

Chapter Five

1. Charles D. Meigs, *Woman: Her Diseases and Remedies*, second edition revised and enlarged (Philadelphia: Lea & Blanchard, 1851), p. 50. This chapter is a compendium of sentimentalist clichés regarding 'true womanhood' and quite unlike the rest of the text which, however mixed with anecdote, does deal with medical issues.
2. Gilbert and Gubar, *The Madwoman in the Attic*, p. 3 and *passim*.
3. Actually, Meigs himself gets caught up in these paradoxes. At the conclusion of his chapter on 'Sexual Peculiarities,' he writes,

> [woman] is unlike man in her fleshly nature, and different from him in her intellectual nature, yet she is a great and predominant Force in the world; physically weaker, yet not less noble; restrained of power, yet the cause and reward of his efforts—requiring his protection, his homage, his love, yet repaying him in the perpetual provocation she offers to noble endeavor. . . .

(Woman: Her Diseases, p. 60)

Meigs has provided, in effect, a gloss for Sigourney's poem.
4. In '"Syllables of Velvet": Dickinson, Rossetti, and the Rhetoric of Sexuality,' Margaret Homans discusses Dickinson's use of the volcano as a symbol of sexual and creative power. See *Feminist Studies* XI (Fall, 1985), p. 591.
5. Rebecca Patterson discusses this relationship in *The Riddle of Emily Dickinson* (Cambridge, Mass.: Houghton Mifflin Company, 1951). I also treat it in *My Life A Loaded Gun*, pp. 55–63.
6. My phrasing has disturbed a number of lesbian readers of the manuscript version of this text. I can only suggest that this reaction may bespeak our own culture's insecurity with the 'small.' At least in Dickinson, 'smaller' is not necessarily lesser. It may, if anything, be more. Cf. 'A solemn thing—it was—I said,' which concludes: 'And then—the size of this/"small" life—/The Sages—call it small—/Swelled—like Horizons—in my/breast—/And I sneered—softly—"small"!' (#271, F,289).
7. This is the single issue that has divided 'straight' and

'lesbian' feminist readings of Dickinson most completely. With the exception of Morris, all the essayists in Juhasz's *Feminist Critics* privilege the Master relationship as do Wolff, Homans, Mossberg and Gilbert and Gubar. The latter, for example, reprint two of the 'Master' letters in the *Norton Anthology of Literature by Women*, but do not include any of Dickinson's letters to Susan. Although Dickinson's relationship with the Master was obviously an important one for her poetry, the fact that we cannot even be sure of its reality should warn critics to scrutinize more carefully those relationships Dickinson is certain to have had. Of these, to judge by duration and number of letters and poems sent, the most important was unquestionably her relationship with her sister-in-law, which covered thirty-six years and elicited 153 known letters and notes, and 276 poems (more than twice the number sent to any other recipient).

8. Morris, '"The Love of Thee",' in Juhasz, *Feminist Critics*, pp. 102–3. In '"Oh, Vision of Language!"': Dickinson's Poems of Love and Death,' Margaret Homans argues that Dickinson offers a 'radical critique' of hierarchy in her love-after-death poems, thereby redeeming her heterosexual poetry. (Juhasz, *Feminist Critics*, p. 117.)

9. Dickinson herself seems to have been aware of the ambiguity. For example, in the fascicle copy of 'A Little East of Jordan,' she wrote 'Signor' over 'Stranger' in a later hand (#59, F,111). Since the former is a term she applies to the Master in other poems, her afterthought belatedly exploits the poem's dual potential.

10. I am thinking here of Barrett Browning's famous assertion of unrestrained love, 'How do I love thee? Let me count the ways,' in *Sonnets from the Portugese*. Through most of this work, however, Barrett Browning's speaker exhibits a sense of parity with her lover that Dickinson rarely approaches in her heterosexual verse. Far more interesting than her imitation of Barrett Browning is Dickinson's ambiguous *identification with* Robert Browning in 'Her— "last Poems",' written to commemorate her female precursor's death: 'What and if ourself a/Bridegroom—/Put her down—in Italy?' (#312, F,602).

11. Homans, '"Oh, Vision",' in Juhasz, *Feminist Critics*,

, p. 125. This is the substance of the argument, pp. 120–32.

12. *New York Times* Book Review (June 26, 1988), p. 42.

13. Helen McNeil, *Emily Dickinson* (New York and London: Pantheon and Virago, 1986), p. 44. The relation between masochism and culturally-constructed 'femininity' has been explored by, among others, Angela Carter in *The Sadeian Woman and the Ideology of Pornography* (New York: Pantheon Books, 1978). At least since de Sade, the image of woman as sexual victim (and victim of her sexuality) has been part of the Western tradition.

14. This poem appears to have become the 'signature' poem for feminist heterosexual readings of the poet. See, for example, the essays by Gilbert, Keller, Mossberg, Homans and Miller in Juhasz's *Feminist Critics*. No other single poem in the canon receives so much attention from these critics. I have discussed the possible reasons for this phenomenon in '"The Pea That Duty Locks: Lesbian and Feminist-Heterosexual Readings of Dickinson's Erotic Poetry,' in *Lesbian Texts and Contexts: Radical Revisions*, edited by Karla Jay and Joanne Glasgow (New York: New York University Press, 1990).

15. According to both Partridge and the *OED* (second edition), 'balls' was not used as a slang term for testicles until the first quarter of the twentieth century. However, Whitman clearly uses it for testicles in *Children of Adam*: 'Hips, hip-sockets, hip-strength, inward and outward round, man-balls, man-root' (section 9) and, given the context, it seems probable that Dickinson was punning here. The contrast in the poem lies, of course, between aggressive male sexuality (sailors, soldiers, Napoleon) and the 'brief campaign of sting and sweet' women offer each other.

16. 'Difference,' we are told, makes meaning possible. But for Dickinson 'difference' lay in her ability to assert the value and significance of sameness, that is, in her desire to articulate a conception of reality different from the phallocentric one which heterosexuality constructed around her. In this reality, self and other are both one and the same. Hence the importance of her 'domestication' of nature, and hence her persistent (also obsessive) use of nature imagery in her homoerotic poetry. When a phallocentric

conception of 'Difference' enters her writing—as it does in
her religious poetry and in her heterosexual love poetry—
the result is violence, as for example, in 'Kill your balm—
and it's Odors bless you—' (#238). Here the speaker-bird
can only sing as it dies, stabbed by the distant Master.
'The difference between Emily Dickinson's envisioning
her love for men and her envisioning her love for women,'
Adalaide Morris writes, 'is radical enough to suggest her
sense of herself as a participant in two separate yet simul-
taneous universes . . . two opposed conceptual realms. . . .
In one the supremacy of the patriarchy . . . in the other, the
implied equality of sisterhood is played out. . . .' ('"The
Love of Thee",' in Juhasz, *Feminist Critics*, p. 103). As I have
tried to demonstrate by the very structure of this book,
these two realms are 'played out' in Dickinson's poetry as
well, through her handling of the lyric genres in which she
worked.
17. Lillian Faderman was the first to point out this ambiguity
    in 'Wild Nights.' 'Emily Dickinson's Homoerotic Poetry,'
    Higginson Journal, XVIII (1978), pp. 19–20.
18. Homans discusses this poem in '"Syllables of Velvet,"' in
    Feminist Studies. Although she sees it as 'subverting' the
    heterosexual tradition, she does not acknowledge its
    homoeroticism or its emphasis on oral sex.
19. In an obvious attempt to evade the homoerotic content,
    critics have read this poem as either one more elegy
    dedicated to Elizabeth Barrett Browning or else as a
    persona poem in which Dickinson writes in the 'hus-
    band's' voice. In either case, however, the poem still
    implies that Dickinson fantasized making love to a
    woman. The homoerotic content has simply been shifted
    to the subtext. See n. 10 above.
20. Dickinson uses 'face' as a code term for the genitals in a
    letter to Judge Otis P. Lord: 'How could I long to give who
    never saw your natures face—' (L,664).
21. Homans, '"Oh, Vision",' in Juhasz, *Feminist Critics*, p. 130.
22. Judy Grahn, *The Highest Apple: Sappho and The Lesbian Poetic
    Tradition* (San Francisco: Spinsters, Ink, 1985), p. 96. Both
    American and British translations of Sappho's poems were
    available during the nineteenth century, and Higginson
    published an essay on Sappho in the *Atlantic Monthly* in

Notes

1871, so it is possible, if not provable, that Dickinson knew the fragment. Dickinson identifies Susan with Heaven in her early letters (see L,208 and 234).

23. Translated by Mary Barnard (Berkeley and London: University of California Press, 1958), no. 34, n.p.

24. Ellen Moers, *Literary Women: The Great Writers* (New York: Oxford University Press, 1985), p. 244.

25. Meigs, *Woman: Her Diseases*, p. 130. Knowledge of the clitoris's role in female eroticism was 'lost' in the course of the nineteenth century as part of a general (politically-motivated) redefining of female sexuality. See Thomas Laqueur, 'Orgasm, Generation, and the Politics of Repro-ductive Biology,' in *The Making of the Modern Body: Sexuality and Society in the Nineteenth Century*, edited by Catherine Gallagher and Thomas Laqueur (Berkeley and London: University of California Press, 1988), pp. 1–41.

26. As noted earlier, Naomi Schor treats the subject of clitoral imagery but only in respect to the use of synecdoche (detail) in male writing. In 'Still Practice, A/Wrested Alphabet: Toward a Feminist Aesthetic' in Benstock, *Feminist Issues*, p. 83, Jane Marcus coins the term *'cliterologos'* to define a female literary tradition, but does not expand upon the point in terms of the clitoral itself. Why the clitoris has suffered this eclipse in the writing of both male *and* female critics is a subject that lends itself too easily to speculation and therefore I will not indulge. However, I would observe that Jane Gallop's recent dismissal of the clitoris as 'the dar-ling of feminist sexology' has not advanced the discussion any further. See *Thinking through the Body* (New York: Columbia University Press, 1989), p. 98. Like many discus-sants of female sexuality, including Luce Irigaray, whom she draws upon heavily, Gallop seems only to conceive of the clitoris as a little (and therefore inadequate) penis.

The *locus classicus* for a discussion of uterine imagery in women's 'art' is Erik Erikson's influential essay 'Woman-hood and the Inner Space,' in *Identity: Youth and Crisis* (New York: W. W. Norton, Inc., 1968), pp. 261–94. In *Through the Flower*, Judy Chicago discusses her develop-ment of vaginal imagery and the empowering effect working with this imagery had on her. *Through the Flower: My Struggle as as Woman Artist*, with an Introduction by

Anaïs Nin, revised and updated (Garden City: Anchor Press, 1982), pp. 51–8 and *passim*.

27. I am fearfully aware that I am treading close to essentialism with these statements, but the prevalence of this kind of imagery in nineteenth-century women poets other than Dickinson leaves me no recourse. Here, for example, is Miss H. F. Gould, speaking in the voice of a crocus: 'I will not despair, nor be idle, nor frown,/Locked in so gloomy a dwelling;/My leaves shall run up, and my roots shall run down,/While the bud in my bosom is swelling' (in Hale, *Flora's Interpreter*, p. 240); and here is Sigourney, reworking the same idea: 'Think'st thou to be conceal'd, thou little seed,/That in the bosom of the earth art cast,/. . ./Unhood thy eyes, unfold thy clasping sheath,/And stir the languid pulses of thy heart' (May 90). While few women poets take their commitment to the small as far as Dickinson did, their obsession with this kind of imagery is hard to deny and suggests that psychologically-speaking they felt very comfortable with it. Further research will be required however to bear this contention—and its implications—out.

28. I am attempting to set limits on this discussion by defining clitoral images as small *and* round. If, however, we use either Moer's images of small objects (*per se*) or Schor's definition of the clitoral as 'detail,' then Dickinson's poetry, in so far as it privileges both smallness and detail, is clitoral throughout.

29. See poem #s 84, 237, 238, 249, 872, 299, 213, 452, 520, 235 and letter #s 209, 233, and 562 (taking 'Bread' as a synonym for 'Loaf'). For another version of 'God gave a Loaf,' substituting 'Berry' for 'Crumb,' see 'Deprived of other Banquet,' #773.

30. Porter, for example, says of this poem that in it '[t]he metaphors of the "Berry of Domingo" and "Torrid Eye" take the place of comprehension.' See *The Modern Idiom*, p. 174. Similarly, Sharon Cameron comments that 'utterance conspires to angle meaning to such a degree that it becomes oblique to the point of invisibility.' See *Lyric Time: Dickinson and The Limits of Genre* (Baltimore and London: Johns Hopkins University Press, 1979), p. 16.

31. I am indebted to Ms Deborah Pfeiffer for calling my attention to this anagram.

32. The appearance of the holograph version of this poem is in itself telling. The paper is folded in two as if for a note, and the poem is written as if it were—in fact—some kind of letter. That is, it is written horizontally, not vertically, in respect to the fold. Dickinson then folded the sheet twice more, writing 'Sue' on the outside flap. Given the manner of presentation—plus the contents—I find it inconceivable that Susan would not have read this poem as being addressed personally to her.
33. Hitchcock, *The Power of Christian Benevolence*, p. 301. The phrase is of course a commonplace.

Conclusion

1. Luce Irigaray, *This Sex Which Is Not One*, translated by Catherine Porter with Carolyn Burke (Ithaca: Cornell University Press, 1985), p. 134.
2. Irigaray, *This Sex*, pp. 24 and *passim*.
3. Irigaray, *This Sex*, p. 134.

List of Poems Cited

List of Poems Cited

List of Poems Cited

Index

218

Index

clitoris, 170
clitoral imagery, 171–3, 212
   n. 28
  in Dickinson, 154–5, 172–9
  in other women poets, 212
   n. 27
Cody John, 191 n. 12
Cooke, Rose Terry, 166 n. 4
Cooper, Mrs James S., 86
'Cousin Robert,' 8

Dana, Mrs William Starr, 199
   n. 155
Darwinism, 79
De Chirico, 34
de Sade, 209 n. 13
Demeter, 89
Dickinson, Austin, 65, 120,
   151, 152, 154, 155, 157
Dickinson, Edward, 94, 187
   n. 12
Dickinson, Edward ('Ned'),
   44, 85, 88–9, 190 n. 4,
   196 n. 1, 204–5 n. 16
Dickinson, Emily Norcross,
   8, 11, 12, 71, 187, n. 12
Dickinson, Lavinia
   ('Vinnie'), 12, 14, 115,
   164
Dickinson, Susan Gilbert, 14,
   17, 21, 40, 58, 59, 99,
   111, 155, 157, 158, 163,
   164–5, 171, 179, 213
   n. 32
Dickinson: The Modern Idiom,
   39
Diehl, Joanne, 118, 191 n. 11,
   195 n. 22
Dobson, Joanne, 185–6 n. 1
Domenichino, 100
Donne, John, 36

Douglas, Ann, 4, 25, 53, 55,
   57, 58, 64, 72, 194 n. 4
Drama of the Gifted Child, The,
   138
Dumont, Henrietta, 94

Eames, Elizabeth J., 56
Easling, Mrs, 3, 6, 9
Eberwein, Jane, 12, 206 n. 29
Edwards, Jonathan, 54–5
Eliot, George, 15
Embury, Emma, 126
Emerson, Ralph Waldo, 36,
   51, 197 n. 10, 197–8,
   n. 12
  Nature, 92–3
  'Rhodora,' 25–7
  The Poet, 108–9, 111–12
Erikson, Erik, 211 n. 26

Female Poets of America, The, 1
*Feminization of American
   Culture, The*, 53
Field, Mrs Thomas P., 84
Finch, Annie, 200 n. 17
*Flora's Interpreter: Or, The
   American Book of
   Flowers and Sentiments*,
   94
*Floral Offering: A Token of
   Affection and Esteem,
   The*, 94
Flynt, Eudocia (Converse),
   100, 167
Follen, Eliza, 56–7
Ford, Emily Ford, 10, 110
Forrer, Richard, 54, 55
Foster, R. S., 55, 64
'Free-bird' poem, 136–7
French, Daniel Chester, 47
Freud, Sigmund, 172

Index